Dynastic Planning

Dynastic Planning

A 7-Step Approach to Family Business Succession Planning and Related Conflict Management

Walid S. Chiniara

BEP BUSINESS EXPERT PRESS

Dynastic Planning: A 7-Step Approach to Family Business Succession Planning and Related Conflict Management

Copyright © Business Expert Press, LLC, 2020.

Cover image licensed by Ingram Image, StockPhotoSecrets.com

Cover and interior design by Exeter Premedia Services Private Ltd., Chennai, India

First published in 2020 by
Business Expert Press, LLC
222 East 46th Street, New York, NY 10017
www.businessexpertpress.com

ISBN-13: 978-1-94999-182-6 (paperback)
ISBN-13: 978-1-94999-183-3 (e-book)

Business Expert Press Entrepreneurship and Small Business Management Collection

Collection ISSN: 1946-5653 (print)
Collection ISSN: 1946-5661 (electronic)

First edition: 2020

10 9 8 7 6 5 4 3 2 1

Printed in the United States of America.

To Erik and Karl

This book is about the sustainability of family business in the hands of the next-generation family business entrepreneurs. It was written with those NextGen in mind:

– You are the future.

– Dream big, be bold, and never fear.

– Also, be respectful of your elders, love your neighbor, stay true to yourselves, work relentlessly, and always strive for excellence.

No one can construct for you the bridge upon which precisely you must cross the stream of life, no one but you yourself alone.

—Friedrich Nietzsche

Abstract

This book is designed to be a guide. It seeks to demystify the journey leading to preserving family legacy.

It is based on the fact that a family business is a partnership among its members, and that the most successful family business succession plan is the one devised by the family itself.

In this book, the author shares his unique experience working with hundreds of business families and next-generation family business entrepreneurs from across the world.

His 7-Step Methodology™ offers an innovative and a systemic approach to family business succession planning and related conflict management. It focuses on the importance of maintaining an open dialogue among family members, and it paves the way to a structured conversation among those interested in achieving an orderly transfer of wealth from one generation to another.

This book further discusses the elements that traditionally cause tensions among partners who happen to be family members, and offers solutions that have been tried and tested over two decades and that are based on real-life examples and success stories.

This book is addressed to families in business looking to start a succession planning conversation, and to family business advisors invited to facilitate such a conversation.

Contents

Contents

Preamble

For many, the concept of a family business is an enigma. For others, it is nothing but a statistic, a phenomenon destined for failure by the third generation.

This may be attributed to the following:

1. Within family businesses, like all aspects of family life, things tend to be conducted behind closed doors. Like an iceberg, only the tiny tip is exposed and open to scrutiny. What you see is often a "home-baked" report devoid of the expertise required of otherwise managed companies or firms.

2. Only a handful of professionals have actually worked directly with families in business, as entry into the inner circle is by invitation only. Very few have been extended such a privilege, as outside intrusion is deemed to be unnecessary and unwelcome.

I am, however, one of those fortunate enough to have been afforded the opportunity.

Today, while I agree that family businesses are facing unprecedented challenges, I find the popular adage "clogs to clogs in three generations" to be outdated (it was first mooted over three centuries ago). Not only is it outdated, it is also incredibly disrespectful to the next generation of family business entrepreneurs (NextGen). If anything, it serves as a self-fulfilling prophecy for the failure of the NextGen. My experience demonstrates that the current NextGen is highly motivated, better educated, and intensely focused on making a successful transition in an increasingly complex and hostile business environment. Passing on the mantle does not destine the business for failure and usually, indeed, is absolutely essential to its very survival. This requires a great leap of faith, then hard work, dedication, and perseverance. For me, every generation is a first generation in its own right (a theory first advocated by James E. Hughes, Jr., Esq.).

The fact of the matter is that the world as we know it has ceased to exist, yielding the way for a new, rocky, and dangerously challenging road toward a new world order.

> *The old order changeth, yielding place to new, And God fulfils himself in many ways, Lest one good custom should corrupt the world.*
> —Alfred, Lord Tennyson, "Idols of the King"

1. Seismic shifts are currently taking place across the globe at an unprecedented level, be it geopolitical, technological, cultural, societal, legal, or regulatory;
2. Family businesses are going through a generational change, and over the next couple of decades trillions of dollars will pass from one generation to another; and
3. People are living longer. NextGen family business entrepreneurs are less inclined to wait patiently in the shadows of their elders until the business is transferred to them. Being educated, autonomous, and ambitious, they have their own visions and seek to pursue their own dreams (while retaining a pride and sense of privilege in their role of maintaining and ensuring the continuance of a family heritage).

These facts are disconcerting because in most countries, family businesses are the backbone of the economy and in many, they are the employer of choice.

Should family businesses collapse, they would jeopardize the societal equilibrium currently in existence. In this regard, their survival in the hands of the NextGen has become, in many respects, a matter of national security.

My Findings

When asked why they would rather set up their own businesses than join the family business, about 90 percent of the NextGen interviewed would cite the lack of a comprehensive succession planning process as their number-one concern. Family feud comes second.

If these matters were remedied, and proper governance systems and frameworks were to be introduced and implemented, approximately

75 percent of those questioned would consider changing their mind, and potentially join the family business.

Unfortunately, over 80 percent of the families interviewed are only just waking up to the challenges ahead and have not yet taken any measures to prepare for the transfer of their wealth to the NextGen. Furthermore, up to 90 percent of those families do not know where or how to start.

For these reasons, I have decided to weigh in on the family business discussion and contribute my insights and experience from working with families in business for the past 23 years.

What This Book Is About

Unfortunately, almost all the mandates I have worked on have had an element of conflict to them. Consequently I have, over the years, become the go-to expert mediator for family business succession planning, but often this resembles "mission impossible" when the underlying dispute has reached a point where my experience and professional input has little impact.

This book is about family business succession planning and associated conflict management. A preemptive strike to avoid disaster.

It is also about preparedness.

The newspapers are littered with examples of family feuds and of family businesses disintegrating for reasons many do not understand.

In my experience, most conflicts that arise in a family business environment find their origin in a sense of injustice family members may feel toward a given situation. Family businesses have their genesis in a loving environment and are driven by a passion to secure family well-being and financial security. This is a strong foundation but will become brittle as the malleable clay that becomes breakable only when the valuable jug has been created.

Examples of situations I have witnessed that have bred such emotions have included:

- Failed investments (largely driven by a minority of family members)
- Dividend payments that have not met expectations

- Remuneration to family member executives deemed to be unjustified by other family members
- Discrimination in the employment of family members (e.g., his son, but not my son)
- Incomplete/inaccurate/absent reporting
- Lack of acknowledgment/recognition/reward for family members who have contributed to the success of the business

Such emotions often surface when I attempt to level the playing field. Only when they are prodded by an "outsider" do the heavily disguised cracks appear, by which time, unfortunately, the wounds have been left to fester and poison family relationships until the pressure becomes too great to contain and an ancestor's dream is inevitably doomed to a painful ending.

What I Hope This Book Will Do/Achieve

Despite the foregoing, I am not a prophet of doom! The purpose of this book is to celebrate families in business, their achievements, and their successes.

It is about the continuity of legacy, and the harmonious and orderly transfer of wealth (whether tangible or intangible, and whether business related or not) into the hands of the NextGen family business owners. These brave people are taking on a mantle which will be fraught with the obstacles and challenges of an inevitably larger family grouping than when the business was started. These new leaders deserve every chance to succeed and this can be achieved only through a properly crafted and carefully managed handing over of the reins.

Throughout this book, the term *family wealth* (referred to by some as patrimony) will be used in its broadest sense. It will transcend the financial aspects of a family business and will include, in addition to financial capital, the human, the intellectual, the spiritual, and the cultural capital that, as a whole, defines the family behind a business. (This definition as well as the terms *my family* and *familiness* that are used in this book are borrowed from the writings of James E. Hughes, Jr., Esq.)

Who is This Book For?

In my opinion, the most successful family business succession plans are those devised by the families themselves.

For this reason, I have written this book first and foremost for the families in business. It is intended to alleviate their fears and introduce them to the benefits of organizing their succession soonest, and if they are not yet ready to pass on the mantle, to at least start thinking of an alternative option. It cannot be said enough:

> *The best time to plant a tree was twenty years ago. The second best time is now.*
>
> —Chinese proverb

It is also addressed to the trusted advisors of families in business, and to those aspiring to serve business families and NextGen family business entrepreneurs.

To the veterans among us, I would be grateful if you could review the contents of this book and share with me your thoughts and your teachings.

To the newcomers to the market, I cannot stress enough the fact that family business advisory is a calling. It is a vocation and not a profession. It is *sui generis,* and it is far from being a hobby. For these reasons, I would strongly recommend that you do your homework and be humble enough to train under a reputable veteran, before aspiring to serve a family in business.

> *If you can, help others; if you cannot do that, at least do not harm them.*
>
> —Dalai Lama

I am an advocate of the ten-thousand-hour rule, so brilliantly developed in *Outliers: the Story of Success,* by Malcom Gladwell. Reading, studying, practicing, and working relentlessly to achieve perfection are the recipe for success.

Reading is an honor and a gift from a warrior or historian who—a decade or a thousand decades ago—set aside time to write. He distilled a lifetime of campaigning in order to have a 'conversation' with you [...] it would be idiotic and unethical to not take advantage of such accumulated experiences. If you haven't read hundreds of books, you are functionally illiterate, and you will be incompetent, because your personal experiences alone aren't broad enough to sustain you.

—James Mattis, in *Call Sign Chaos*

Read 500 pages like this every day. That's how knowledge works. It builds up, like compound interest. All of you can do it, but I guarantee not many of you will do it.

—Warren Buffett

Sharing My Perspective

I have approached family business advisory from a lawyer's prism, with a dose of common sense, problem solving, and critical thinking.

I view my role to include the following:

- Helping patriarchs/matriarchs sleep better at night, knowing their affairs are in order and their legacy is in good hands
- Helping siblings/cousins find common ground, and agree to a sustainable roadmap for the future
- Helping put in place the foundations for an enduring family business

This approach will help save/create jobs in a highly insecure and volatile global world.

This book is about the lessons I have learned over the past two decades.

It will clarify what I believe planning a succession within a family business context truly entails.

It will demystify the concepts surrounding a family business ecosystem and it will discuss the stages that make up a family business succession journey.

Most importantly, this book is about giving and taking. It is about consensus building, and about the journey leading to devising a common project (partnership) among the owners of a family business.

In this book, I will share my approach to family business succession planning and the 7-Step Methodology™ that I have developed to accompany business families throughout their succession planning journey.

For those who are wondering, this book will not discuss legal, tax, or management consulting remedies, nor will it address estate planning, trust, tax, or other financial or scientific structures, as many others before me have done. While they are important, it is my view that these aspects are redundant without a solution to the otherwise more complex and nontangible underlying issues.

Furthermore, this book will not discuss live cases I have worked on, for two reasons:

1. I am not good at case studies, nor am I good at sugar-coating words. I have spent the best part of the past 23 years in the trenches practicing what I preach. This book offers solutions and tools I have found to be effective over the years. For real-life case study examples and war stories, I would recommend that you attend family business conferences, and read books, business newspapers, and university-generated papers and studies.

2. I am of the belief that any discussion of live cases will be disconcerting for my families, and a breach of fiduciary duty on my part. Family business disputes are as many and varied as car crashes. The "satnav" advice to avoiding them is a constant.

As such, succession planning as addressed in this book is the prerequisite and the foundation to the "rest" that will ultimately follow.

An Invitation to Start a Conversation

While the 7-Step Methodology™ has served me and *my families* well over the years, this methodology should not be viewed as a magic solution for a successful succession plan, nor a miracle solution against all family feuds.

The application of the 7-Step Methodology™ is influenced by a multitude of factors and variables and can by no means be viewed as a guarantee of outcomes.

Family business succession planning is multidimensional and, in many cases, multicultural. This book barely scratches the surface. Every family and each family member should be addressed on a case-by-case basis and the contents of this book is not a substitute for communication. Indeed, the intended outcome is to increase such communication. To ensure the success of their endeavor, families need to engage in a conversation. They need to discuss and agree on what they really aspire to achieve, and how they will go about it. Communication is the prerequisite to introducing structures and systems.

A family business is not built to fit in a structure—rather, a structure is built to fit a family business.

Acknowledgments

The past 23 years and this book in particular would not have been possible without the support of my family and my friends, as well as the members of my team who stood by my side all these years. They helped me to shape my thoughts and, more importantly, they helped me to stay the course when things got tough.

A special thank you goes to Yasmine Omari for her steadfast support throughout the writing of this book, to Colin Howie for his courage and patience going over my prose and for his help making it more readable, and to Carol Anderson for her proofreading of the text.

Introduction

When faced with conflict, many families look for shortcuts: a "standard family charter" and a set of "best practice" rules they can "take home" to dictate and "impress" on their family members.

Many among those fall prey to the hobbyists who promise them the moon and instead deliver grief and pain.

In my opinion, in family business, there are no shortcuts, there are no standard templates, or "one-size-fit-all" family charters, and there are no "best practice" rules that apply to "succession planning."

Also, there is no such thing as a succession plan or family charter (also called a family constitution, family protocol, family book, etc.) that can be imposed or enforced on a family.

A family charter is nothing but an instrument (preferably a written one) that summarizes the rules of engagement that members of a family who are in business together collectively ascribe to in pursuit of a common project.

It is the culmination of a long journey a family in business embarks on, to decide if (1) all (or some) of its members want to unite around one common project (the *family business*), and (2) if yes, under what conditions they are willing to do so.

Succession planning is not, as many would want to believe, a mere process. It is rather a journey that starts, in some cases, from the cradle, and that can take a lifetime to complete. It grows organically and develops at the pace of the slowest family member.

The journey leading to the "construction" of a family charter is personal. The more time and effort a family invests in such a journey, the higher the odds that it will end up with a workable and sustainable family charter.

It is more about the people behind the business than it is about the business itself, or even the money the business generates.

Because a succession planning journey is fettered with "emotions," families often choose to distance themselves from the exercise and prefer to engage the services of a third-party facilitator whose principal role is to ask the hard questions and facilitate the dialogue among family members.

Where applicable, a facilitator would sometimes hold the pen on behalf of the family.

Ideally, the family members would be the ones who write their own family charter.

Either way, a family charter is written by the family, for the family. It must be owned by them and tailor-made to meet their specific needs and circumstances.

Experience has shown that passing on a business from one generation to another, in an orderly fashion, requires sacrifice, trust, love, and forgiveness.

Some families choose to do it preemptively—planning in advance. Others, and unfortunately these being the majority, do it reactively, when an event forces the process.

It is always more efficient (time, money, and effort) to prevent, than to cure.

An ounce of prevention is worth a pound of cure.

—Benjamin Franklin

Structure of the Book

I approached this book keeping in mind the business families I have worked with and the various tragedies many among them have sadly experienced or are currently experiencing.

More often than not, my work has touched upon succession planning and the use of tools to ensure the Strength, Security, and Sustainability for a family-owned business (what I call the "3S" insurance policy). Simultaneously, however, most of my work has also touched upon the subject of conflict and conflict management.

Experience has shown that there is no one-standard-fits-all succession planning strategy. What works for one family, may not work for another.

There is only one strategy per family, and every family has its own strategy.

The 7-Step Methodology™ rests on three pillars, as follows:

- The **Journey** that takes a family from the present to the future;
- The **Hard Work** required to get that family there; and
- The **Communication** platforms that a family needs to build and maintain to safeguard peace and harmony at home.

This book follows this reasoning, and is divided into two parts, as follows:

Part 1 comprises three chapters:
Chapter I: Family Business Succession Planning: The Journey
Chapter II: Succession Plan Conditions of Success: The Hard Work
Chapter III: The Glue That Ensures the Stability, the Security, and the Sustainability of the Family Business: Communication

Part 2 comprises three chapters:
Chapter I: Concepts Underpinning a Family Charter
Chapter II: Typical Table of Contents
Chapter III: Select Provisions of a Family Charter—Annotated

For me, a family charter is a means to an end, not an end in itself. I would recommend that families focus on the journey leading to a family charter rather than on the charter itself. A charter merely documents what has been agreed to between the parties.

The stakes are too high, and failure is not an option.

Yesterday is gone. Tomorrow has not yet come. We have only today. Let us begin.

—Mother Theresa

PART 1

Family Conversations Matter

If I had only one hour to save the world, I would spend fifty-five minutes defining the problem, and only five minutes finding the solution.
—Albert Einstein

In the same vein, 91.66 percent of the process of a succession planning journey is framing the issues, while the remaining 8.34 percent would be to devise the ensuing family charter.

Family Business Succession Planning: The Journey

Family Business Succession Planning

Family business succession planning is about the transmission of something by someone to someone else. It is also about:

A: Giving and taking, and

B: Building a common project

Going from point A to point B is a journey filled with pitfalls and challenges.

I hear many seniors giving their juniors the following test:

This exercise is for you. We would like you to work with the advisors, and be as forthcoming as possible, for your own good. We will be in the next room. Should you have any questions, just let us know what you want, and we will make sure it happens.

While this attitude is graceful, it does not serve the purpose.

Giving and taking is not about seniors vs. juniors. It is about seniors + juniors.

It is about the family at large. The people behind the business.

Seniors and juniors must go through the journey together, at the same time, and around the same table.

The 7-Step Methodology™ has proven useful in helping family members to align with a common project and, as such, devise a roadmap for a successful partnership.

This methodology was developed with the following three recurring concerns in mind:

- *What* is succession planning in a family business context all about?
- *Who* is transferring *what* to *whom*?
- *Me* as a member of the family, where do I fit? What's in it for me? What is my role?

The 7-Step Methodology™ is illustrated in Figure 1.1, below.

Figure 1.1

Structure of Chapter I

Chapter I of the process is intended to be interactive.

It is divided into seven sections, one for each of the seven steps illustrated above.

At the end of each section, I have shared a series of exercises. They are intended to bring the 7-Step Methodology™ to real-life scenarios.

The activities proposed are intended to be group activities, preferably facilitated by an expert family business advisor. They are meant to break the ice, build trust, and encourage interaction and dialogue. Done properly, they will help participants open up to one another and get to know one another better.

Please keep in mind that these activities are not designed as hard and fast rules to cover every contingency. They are examples that I have personally developed based on the needs of *my families*. Develop your own. Go with the flow. Family business succession planning is not about the advisor; it is about the family. They are the ones in charge. They are the ones who will sink or swim by their interpretation and execution of these methods.

The Guiding Principles

The 7-Step Methodology™ has been built with the following 3S's in mind:

1. The **strength** of a business family is dependent upon the (i) strength of the bond among its family members and (ii) culture of privacy the family develops and nurtures;
2. The **security** of a family business depends to a great extent on the implementation of comprehensive and scalable governance systems and processes, in the interest of the family and the business; and
3. The **sustainability** of a family business is defined by the ability and the will of the (i) senior members of the family to transfer their wealth to their NextGen, in an orderly fashion; and (ii) NextGen to actively receive the wealth from their seniors, and in turn, plan the future transfer to their own NextGen.

Step 1—Know to Give and Take

Succession planning is where giving and taking meet (*"un rendez-vous du donner et du recevoir,"* an expression coined by President Léopold Sédar Singhor, of the Académie Française.)

The Art of Transferring

There is nothing more frustrating for a son or a daughter than to hear their father/mother tell them: "I built this for you. One day this will all be yours."

Parents build a business for themselves. They are the ones who develop a passion for what they do. They are the ones who attend the gala dinners and have their pictures on the cover of business magazines. They are the ones who get all the awards, and who shake hands with the heads of state, ministers, and other government officials. Ultimately the parents, as founders, receive all the gratification they want from their business.

However, at one point in time, responsible patriarchs/matriarchs need to ask themselves the hard questions:

"What do I do with all this? Do I pass it on? Do I sell it? Do I keep it for myself or *que sera sera*?"

If the conclusion is *to pass it on*, then what happens next? How is this achieved in an orderly and non-disruptive manner?

Succession planning in a family business context refers to the transfer of the "baton" (some would say the "flame") from one generation to the next.

Personally, I would use the term flame, but only if I am confident that the transferors and the transferees are indeed in sync. Otherwise, inevitably, one party will get their fingers burnt in the process. Often, a father's dream has nothing to do with his son/daughter's dream. In this case, the term baton or mantle becomes more appropriate.

The act of transferring something to someone else requires both the transferor and the transferee to put themselves in a certain mind frame.

Succession planning refers to the three elements comprising a family business:

Ownership + Shareholding + Management.

Beyond the transfer of shares and the financial interest in the family business, there is the transfer of the (non-tangible) "spirit" of ownership, which is integral to any given family business.

It is often assumed that the transfer of the "spirit" of ownership is something that happens by osmosis, or perhaps something that is hereditary. It is believed that by the mere fact of being born into "our family," children automatically inherit their parents' business mindset and will pick up the traits and core values of "our family."

On the face of it, this is perhaps a realistic expectation on the basis that "blood is thicker than water," but in reality, there are many practicalities and external influences that impact this process.

Again, osmosis is not a passive action. For osmosis to occur, and for the NextGen to become assimilated with the thoughts, culture, ideas, values, and vision of their parents and grandparents, they must spend time together and interact with one another.

With the demands of day-to-day life, this time becomes scarce and often falls low on the list of priorities. Today's social media has undermined considered opinion, the mobile phone has encouraged casual communication at the expense of necessary communication, and texting has largely overtaken the bonding qualities of conversation between friends and within families.

Investing in the Transfer of the "Spirit" of Ownership

The stakeholders of successful family businesses must be encouraged to view succession planning as an investment. They invest time, effort, and money to achieve a smooth and equitable transition.

In exchange, they expect a proportionate return on their investment (ROI).

Studies have shown that where an end result or reward is identified, people are much more likely to allocate time and effort as an investment in any given task.

The ROI for a business family in undertaking a succession planning journey is ultimately the success and continuity of the business in the hands of the next generation. As ROIs go, this is a fairly abstract measure or indicator, as this success and continuity are notoriously difficult to quantify and monitor. Success is often perceived not to be measurable prior to the completion of the succession. This is a misconception in the notion of succession planning. Excuse the cliché, but the act of succession is not an event that takes place overnight; rather, it is a journey. That being said, it is human nature to want tangible and concrete targets, and to this end, it is important to introduce key performance indicators (KPIs) to monitor and measure success and progress during the journey.

In traditional discourse, the notion of succession planning is predominantly associated with the transfer of power, and is approached from a leadership and management perspective as a process for *identifying* and *developing* successors to replace their seniors following their retirement or departure. Ownership, however, is often taken for granted, and not much attention is given to it.

Experience has shown that in a family business environment, no matter is too insignificant and no individual should be taken for granted. KPIs should be introduced across the board and used as a monitoring tool.

KPIs could also apply to *transferring* ownership and the related "spirit" of ownership, and to the vital *preparation of* future owners for their impending role.

KPIs can also be used as a tool to measure "what's in it for me" for a family member. "Am I (my achievements, my ideas, my family, my children, my importance) being acknowledged, recognized, and taken seriously?"

There Are Two Main Types of Succession Planning

Succession planning can be *preemptive* (during the lifetime of the individual(s) being succeeded) or *reactive* (following a crisis or following the death of the individual(s) being succeeded), though arguably, reactive succession is not necessarily a plan. Reactive succession occurs when little heed has been taken of the modern adage "to fail to prepare is to prepare to fail."

Typically, a family business succession planning exercise begins when the current active owner(s) of a given business wish(es) to hand over ownership and/or management to the NextGen, in an orderly fashion. This may be at a time when the incumbent owner, who may have had success early on in their family business enterprise, wishes to step down while they still have time to enjoy the fruits of their labor. Alternatively, it may be when they are aware that they are reaching the end of their business life and realize that succession will become necessary.

In some cases, however, a succession plan is triggered following the occurrence of a major crisis, such as a family feud, a dramatic loss of capital, or the death of a patriarch or a key family member.

In any event, the passing on of a family business and the agreement to take over a family business is always a leap of faith for all parties involved. A founder passes on the business with the hope that the NextGen can effectively take it over and run with it. Likewise, the NextGen takes over a business with the expectation that they can do justice to the business and to their predecessors, preserve it, and take it to the next level.

> *I don't know what the future may hold, but I know who holds the future.*
>
> —Ralph Abernathy

In general terms, a transfer usually puts into play five elements, as follows:

1. The parties to the transfer: the transferor(s) and the transferee(s)
2. The object of the transfer
3. The relationship among the transferee(s)
4. The relationship between the transferee(s) and the object being transferred
5. The relationship between the transferor(s) and the transferee(s), post transfer

Walid's Insights

Often, in the case of a founder, the business is their first-born. The founder started it from scratch, knows every single nut and bolt that went into it, and nurtured it. The founders know the first employees they hired who are no longer just employees, but rather companions throughout the life of the business. During this journey they have failed together, and succeeded together. They became family.

To separate the founders of a business from their "baby" is a difficult task. It is like taking a part of their identity away from them.

Also, asking a founder to take a back seat, and withdraw from the business is viewed by many as a death sentence. The clock is ticking …

"Are you saying my good years are behind me"; "No one other than me can manage this business"; "The clients know me"; "The banks and the suppliers know me"; "Why do you think they keep on supporting us"; "Where were you when I started this business"; "You just graduated from school, what do you know"; "I am up at 5 am and behind my desk at 6:00. You wake up at 9:00; business cannot be run like that."

… are all things that come up in the conversation.

An integral part of a succession planning process is aligning and managing expectations.

Letting Go

It takes two to tango.

It takes a giver and a receiver, a transferor and a transferee.

In most of the cases we encountered, the transferor is a senior family member who either founded (or purchased) the business themselves or inherited it from their predecessors, looked after it, and took it to (what they perceive to be) the next level.

The Motions

At the beginning of a process, it is normal to see the parties to a transfer come to the table with some apprehension.

Some are more hostile than others.

It is customary to see a dialogue start as a "tug of war," where each one of the parties starts from a certain position and refuses to "give in" (see Figure 1.2).

Donor/Giver/Testator   Recipient/Beneficiary/Heir

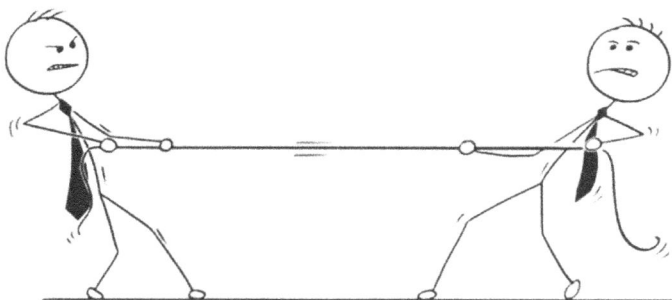

Figure 1.2

Emotions tend to run high and sometimes a "perceived concession" is viewed as a "personal affront."

Figure 1.2 depicts the situation in which some parties find themselves at the beginning of the succession planning exercise.

Slowly, they are encouraged to move from a "pull and give" attitude to "cooperation": in other words, from a tug of war to a relay race (see Figure 1.3).

Figure 1.3

In a relay race, the transferor, at first, holds the baton and slowly lets go of it and passes it to the transferee. Both the transferor and the transferee need to prepare for the moment when the baton will actually be handed over.

Preparation takes place at both levels, mental and physical (see Figure 1.4).

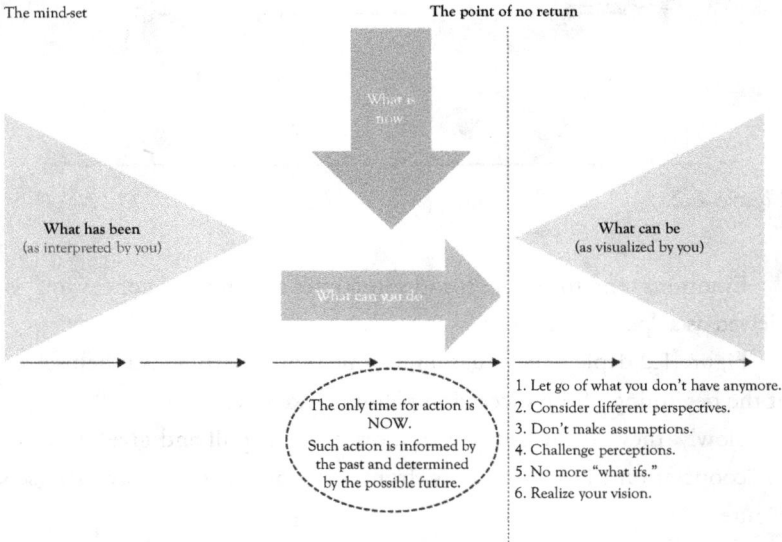

The mind-set   The point of no return

What is now

What has been
(as interpreted by you)

What can you do

What can be
(as visualized by you)

The only time for action is NOW.
Such action is informed by the past and determined by the possible future.

1. Let go of what you don't have anymore.
2. Consider different perspectives.
3. Don't make assumptions.
4. Challenge perceptions.
5. No more "what ifs."
6. Realize your vision.

Figure 1.4

In addition, expectations, on both sides, need to be managed adequately.

Between the perceived "perfect" *replica* of the founder to an "acceptable" replacement that is not the founder, there is a whole world to cross. For a father to pass on the baton to a son, for example, it takes wisdom and courage. From a "son" to an "equal," there is a big step to climb. Incomplete preparation for this event may result in the baton being dropped and other runners in the field (the competition) holding the advantage.

Keep in mind that a father watched his son being born. He has seen him grow up, fall, stand up, make mistakes ... and suddenly, for a father to see his son graduate into real life and behave as his equal requires a major adjustment.

In a relay race, the transferor runs alongside the transferee, for a brief moment, to ensure that the transferee has reached the optimum speed and has taken hold of the baton firmly. This is the moment when transferors reach the maximum level of comfort and feel they are ready to let go of the baton for good. They then start to reduce their speed, and eventually stop running, while watching the transferee do their best, and in turn, prepare to pass on the baton to the next transferee (see Figure 1.5).

Figure 1.5

This requires teamwork. It requires all the members of the team to trust one another. Trust the determination of others to win for the team and trust the ability of others to perform as best as they can. This requires the team to train and get to know one another. They must get to know one another's strengths and weaknesses, accept them and use them in everyone's best interests.

When building a relay race team, no one should accept to add a friend's son or daughter for the sake of pleasing their friend. They should only select individuals who are qualified and can add value and ultimately lead them to success. Everyone wants winners on the team: winners who know what is at stake, who want to be there, and who want to win, not only for themselves, but for the team.

A trophy won by the team is shared equally by all its members.

The move from an antagonistic mindset to a collaborative one is the art of the game. Choosing the right coach will make all the difference.

Every interaction/transaction between a "giver" and a "taker" starts with each party bringing differing views, skills, desires, and needs.

Transferors cannot force their business or their money on an unwilling transferee, and transferees cannot regard transferors with impatience, waiting for the cataclysmic event or praying for the demise of the transferor, so that they can inherit their business or their money.

A winning transfer can take place only if there is a meeting of the minds between transferors and transferees.

The following ought to happen in parallel, for a transfer to take place in an orderly fashion.

Transferors Are Expected To:

1. Reach a state of mind where they are convinced that it is time for them to move on, and they are ready to groom a successor, be it a family member or a third-party executive, and
2. Identify a mental date or conditional event/situation where they are comfortable leaving the business (physically or virtually), and not permitting any change to that determination.

Transferees Are Expected To:

1. Go the extra mile prior to the transfer and prove that they have an unrelenting desire to run the business. That they love the business as much, if not more than the transferor, and that they will take care of it, and nurture it as much as he/she did, and even more.
2. Show that they are qualified and have acquired the skillset necessary to take over and add value to the business.

In a nutshell, transferors will not hand over to the transferees unless and until the transferees take ownership of the wealth being transferred, and demonstrate leadership.

As you may have noted, most, if not all, the elements discussed above are subjective and cannot be measured against any tangible benchmark. They are a matter of sensibility on both sides of the equation, and only words and deeds can help raise the level of comfort between transferor and transferee.

While some of the emotions may be impossible to express in writing or to define in legal terms, the underlying "spirit" needs to transpire and be recognized by all parties.

In some cases, the patriarchs are often perceived to be larger than life, based on all they have achieved during their tenure. When this happens, the NextGen tends to start the dialogue on the back foot.

This is where a neutral, third-party facilitator may be able to add value.

This intervention will help bridge the gap between the generations and facilitate the dialogue between seniors and juniors, and among juniors in a sibling or cousin consortia.

Walid's Insights

In many cases, seniors/founders often look for clones of themselves. It takes them a while to accept the fact that such "creatures" do not exist and that something needs to give from their side.

The Alternative

In some cases, the transferor and the transferee are unable to align or see eye to eye. The parties reach a stalemate; a dead end.

Neither the transferor is ready or willing to transfer, nor the transferee ready and able to take over.

In this case, if even the third-party mediation fails, there is not much else that can be done. The parties would need to come to terms with the fact that they are not ready to embark on the succession planning process in its traditional sense, or that perhaps they should either postpone the exercise, or look for an alternative solution.

The current owners of the business would need to go back to the drawing board and work with the NextGen to figure out what to do next.

There are always solutions for such cases; for example:

- Ring-fencing the business and appointing a nonfamily executive to take over the management, or
- Selling the business to a third party, cashing in, and eventually setting up something else with the money received.

For some, this may sound like a sorry end to the family business, or like a sign of failure.

On the contrary, I find this to be a sign of maturity. It is a smart move on the part of the family, and a way to preserve its long-term legacy, preserve jobs, and give the business a new lease on life, even if it is in the hands of someone else.

Giving and Taking Activity

Giving and Taking Activity [1]

List *all* the transferor(s)/giver(s)/testator(s).

Giving and Taking Activity [2]

List *all* the recipients.

List the current recipients (those for whom this succession planning exercise is intended).

List the potential future recipients (heirs of tomorrow). Pay special attention to those who may have an unexpected claim on any part of the business through marriage or hidden family connection.

Giving and Taking Activity [3]—For the Receivers(s)

Put yourself in the shoes of the giver and list the reasons why a giver would be ready to let go, and the reasons why they would not (see Figure 1.6).

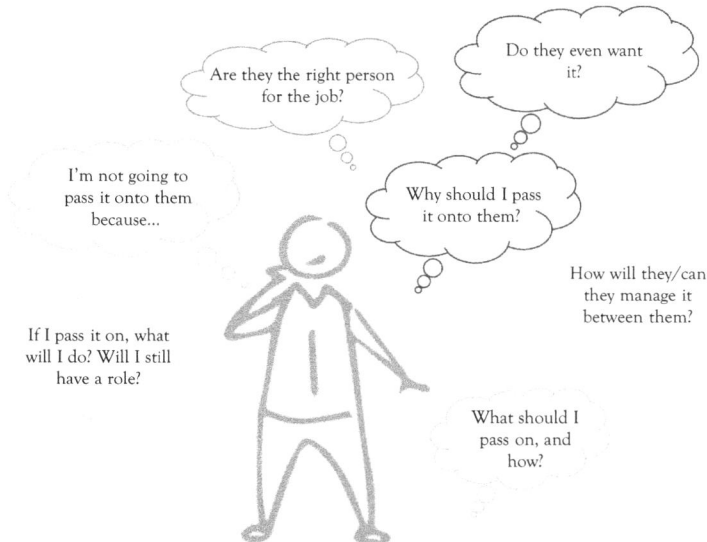

In their shoes: The transferor/giver/testator

Are they the right person for the job?

Do they even want it?

I'm not going to pass it onto them because...

Why should I pass it onto them?

How will they/can they manage it between them?

If I pass it on, what will I do? Will I still have a role?

What should I pass on, and how?

Figure 1.6

It is important to do this exercise for each giver. They may not all have the same objective or the same mindset (see Figure 1.7).

Figure 1.7

Giving and Taking Activity [4]—For the Giver(s)

Put yourself in the shoes of the transferee, and list the motivations why a transferee would be in a position to receive, and the reasons why they would not (see Figure 1.8).

Figure 1.8

It is important to do this exercise for each recipient. They may not all have the same objective or the same mindset (see Figure 1.9).

Figure 1.9

Giving and Taking Activity [5]—The Six-Circle Model

There are cases where I have found it difficult to start a conversation with certain family members.

I developed the following six-circle model to get the ball rolling and get people to focus on the important subjects (see Figure 1.10). I found this tool to be almost entirely representative of the topics families in business typically discuss at the dinner table.

It places the family (and *you*) in the center of the debate and deals with topics everyone can understand and relate to.

I found it to be a great ice-breaker that helps initiate the conversations.

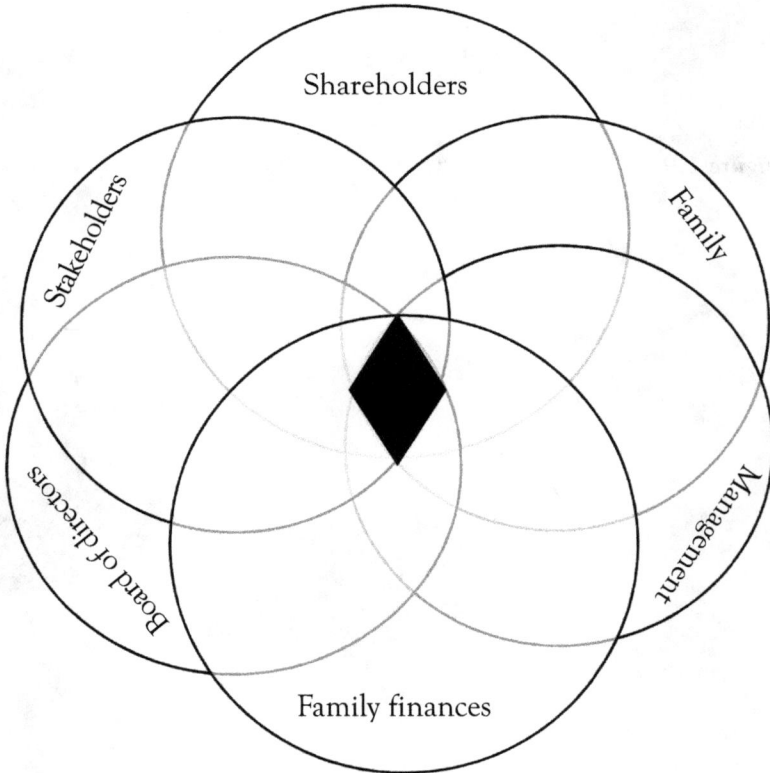

Figure 1.10

As a tool, the six-circle model will greatly help the parties involved to:

- Pinpoint exactly:
  - Where each issue raised by the family sits
  - What role each family member plays
  - What motivates and interests them the most
- Identify individual roles and the role each individual wishes to play in the future shape of the business
- Define the boundaries each should respect, and the job description of each

For the purposes of this activity, the diamond in the middle of the six-circle model is meant to represent the centralization of powers in the hands of one individual, usually the founder, in the case of a first-generation family business.

In a centralized system, the founder (traditionally a patriarch) is omnipresent and becomes the center of gravity of "his" family business.

When he "retires," he is replaced by a successor, hopefully a group of individuals, as opposed to just one individual, thus allowing for less autocracy, and more "democracy."

Even a democracy requires an individual, an elected leader, to ensure that democracy is maintained. It is a contradiction, but anarchy leading to inevitable collapse would be the outcome of a loose family "committee" governing a successful enterprise.

As you do not have one standard form of "democracy," it becomes imperative to define one that suits the needs and the interests of those who will live by it.

Some families are preemptive and start preparing for such a moment well in advance. Others, unfortunately most, procrastinate and delay the inevitable indefinitely.

Some people talk of retirement, and never retire. Others don't even think of retirement and believe that the world will cease to exist without them. Many die on the job and neglect to organize their affairs in advance. Families end up with a crisis on their hands, launching a potential tragedy, for both the family and the business.

Relationships among individuals are complex and reflect the interplay between the two elements that define them: reason and emotions.

Note: Some people may find themselves sitting in more than one "box" or assigned more than one function. The purpose of this activity is to define the boundaries and assign roles for each family member. It is possible that one family member can be assigned multiple roles.

It is one of the hardest activities and the one that requires the most time and effort to complete.

We purposely refrained from labeling the boxes and showing the various options and alternatives. We prefer the family to use its imagination and tailor-make its answers, as it sees fit.

There are no right or wrong answers. They are all valid, as long as they represent reality.

Steps 2 to 6 will further help shape solutions to fit the needs of the family and its members.

Step 2—Know Your Family

In these pages, we refer often to the expression "the people behind the business." These are none other than the family members.

For some, the answer may be obvious, but for others, it may not be.

When embarking on a succession planning journey, it is important to start with the basics.

Who Is Who, and Who Is Transferring What to Whom

When transferring something to someone else, it is crucial to identify who's who, who does what, and what is being transferred. In such instances, precision and certainty are paramount, as any hint of uncertainty can often trigger reactions that have the potential to destabilize the whole process.

The following three steps help put things in perspective:

- Drawing a family tree
- A walk down memory lane
- Calling things by their name

Family Trees

This is a fun exercise that could be entrusted to the younger members of the family.

They would enjoy building a family tree and piecing together the pieces. They would list the family members and figure out their dates of birth, marriage, divorce, and death, where applicable; the names of the spouses, and the children and grandchildren (see Figure 1.11). Each young member will eventually find out where they stand in the family tree and their place in the hierarchy.

Family business advisors tend to use genograms, a science borrowed from the medical world, in drawing family trees. They give a snapshot of the family and allow analysts to identify trends, behaviors, and triangulations.

We tend to ask families to draw a family tree incorporating three to four generations.

At a minimum, next to the name of the individual mentioned in the genogram, we would need to gather the following information: age, date of birth, education, marriage, spouse's first and maiden name, divorce, accidents, death (where applicable), professional activity, and any other information that could become useful for the purposes of the discussions taking place.

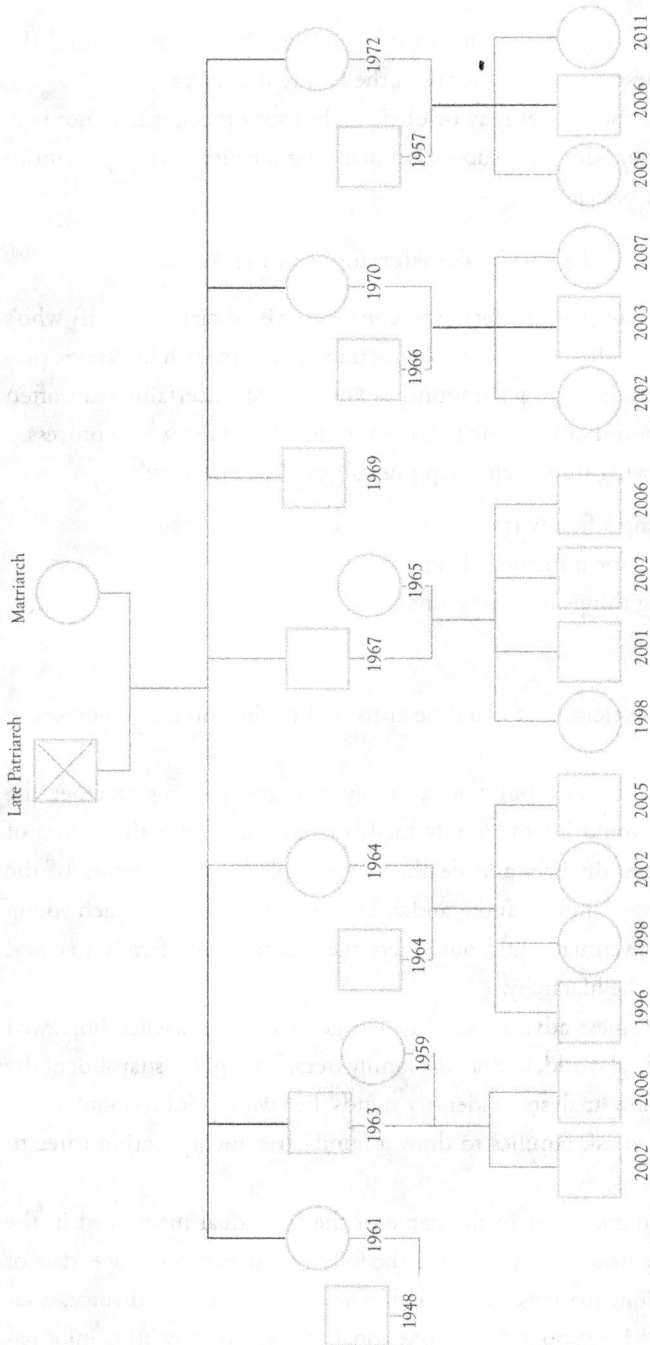

Figure 1.11

This family tree is an example of a family that comprises the following:

Generation 1 comprises a father and a mother. In many cases, we have dealt with families where the patriarch/matriarch has married more than once, and where he/she has children from different spouses.

Males are represented by squares, and females by circles.

In the example above, Generation 2 includes 4 women and 3 men.

Generation 3 comprises 16 grandchildren, who are expected in turn to get married and found their own families, thus resulting in the multiplication of the number of family members at Generation 4, and beyond.

If each grandchild marries once, and has two children, Generation 4 will comprise 32 individuals. We can multiply the numbers as we go on.

In this example, we note that:

The eldest daughter is married and has no children.

Son No. 3 is unmarried and has no children.

Some among the siblings have two children, others have three or four.

This is some of the key information one may identify by simply looking at a genogram. One may push the analysis further and discuss the relationships among family members to identify affinities, and perhaps the lack thereof. After all, if these individuals are called upon to become partners in a business, it would be interesting to identify how they would get along, and if not, how to preempt any hostility or animosity between them, in the interest of the family, or, on the contrary, how to manage affinities between people and protect the weak from the more powerful.

Now, imagine a genogram representing a family comprising 118 members.

Getting to understand a family tree is a first step in a long journey. The history of a family defines that family, and the history of an individual defines that individual.

Imagine a patriarch who has been married three times, and has children from his three wives. This exercise would be undoubtedly more complex in societies that permit multiple spouses or where children are born out of wedlock to one of the family members.

This would result in three groups of siblings, each having the same father, but a different mother, which presents its own set of facts and relationships to deal with.

For example, we learned that in most cases where you have situations similar to this one, the siblings from the same mother or "branch" tend to be closer with their "full" siblings than with their "half-brothers" and "half-sisters."

Each mother raises her children differently, transferring her own "values system," culture, and even language, if it so happens that she is from a different country or different continent.

This *multiculturalism* under the same roof tends to create diversity and wealth. It can also trigger rivalry and jealousy among the siblings.

Getting two individuals to see eye to eye is difficult enough. However, getting 20, 30, or even 118 people to agree a common project and to buy into a common vision is close to mission impossible. Ground rules must be quickly agreed on and established, and for this, an outside arbitrator is key.

Family Structures

A family genogram would comprise at a minimum three categories of family members:

- Immediate family members: Father, mother, and their children;
- In-laws: Spouses and members of their own family tree (their ancestors, parents, siblings, cousins, and so on); and
- Extended family members: Uncles, aunts, cousins, and so on.

This is the reason why drawing a family genogram and identifying who's who in this tree, the origins of each individual, and his/her life cycle are paramount to understanding families and to helping them craft a path for the future.

Calling Things by Their Name

As mentioned above, it is important, early in the exercise, to define who's who, who owns what, and who does what.

Each such element would define the rights and obligations of the individuals involved and would go directly toward affecting one's self-esteem, one's sense of responsibility, and buy-in.

We have noticed that in some families, family members often forget who they are, their place in the family tree, what role they play or should play, and what are their rights and obligations.

More importantly, most forget their boundaries and their limitations.

We have seen elder brothers assume a father's role and abuse their dominant position. Younger siblings would complain that even when they reach the age of 50 or 60, their elder brother would scold or reprimand them as if they were still in their teens, and sometimes in the presence of their spouses or their children.

Others would complain that the elder brother would decide unilaterally how much each of his siblings should receive in annual dividends.

We even had cases where an elder brother would dictate where his brother or sister would spend their summer holidays with their spouses and families, and where they would live or what car they would drive.

Know Your Family Activity

Know Your Family Activity [1]—Construct Your Family Tree/Genogram Activity

Based on your knowledge of the family, and on the model provided in Figure 1.11, construct a genogram of your family showing, at a minimum, the last three generations (see Figure 1.12).

The basic principles for constructing a genogram are as follows:

- Males are shown as squares and females as circles
- The eldest generation should be located at the top, and the youngest at the bottom
- Birth and death years are usually listed around the individual's name, along with any other pertinent information relating to that person

Mapping the family

Founding generation/G1   □   ○

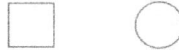

G2

G3

G...

Figure 1.12

Know Your Family Activity [2]—The Wider Family Members

When mapping your genogram, it is critical to include spouses and non-bloodline family members and to consider their impact on the relationships and dynamics within the family. It is also important to determine the extent to which you wish to include them with respect to matters that affect the family business from a family perspective.

Walid's Insights

We have found that sometimes there is an "us and them" mentality when it comes to matters relating to in-laws. Some families choose not to bring them into the fold and to not give them a voice in relation to wider family affairs.

We find this to be influenced and sometimes encouraged by the literature floating around.

Our experience has shown that the strength of a given family is dependent on the human capital representing said family. In-laws may, in certain cases, be viewed as an added value, if they have something positive to contribute to the wealth of the family.

Do keep in mind that inevitably, by virtue of their position within the family as a spouse or a parent (father or mother) of a family member, in-laws have a certain degree of influence, whether you choose to include them or not.

Before excluding them, as a matter of principle, we would recommend that the family weigh the pros and cons of including or excluding in-laws from the equation. You will be surprised by what you may discover. We have seen in-laws more faithful and more passionate about certain businesses than the own children of the founders. Why exclude them to the benefit of a third-party "mercenary"?

We find sometimes that including them turns out to be beneficial and creates an environment of inclusion and transparency. The value that these spouses have added to the marriage would often offer equal added value in the family business.

Know Your Family Activity [3]—Family History, A Walk Down Memory Lane

If you want to know the future, look at the past.

—Albert Einstein

We use the family tree to get to know more about each family member.

Invite each family member to share a *curriculum vitae* (CV).

Be prepared to see something different to what you would otherwise see in the corporate world. The CV will undoubtedly cover topics such as:

- Affiliations (the daughter/son of …)
- Siblings
- Cousins
- Marital status (spouse, children, and so on)
- Upbringing (place of birth, schooling, friends, travels, interests, affinities, interests, hobbies, and so on)
- Work experience (languages, dreams, ambitions, first job, professional progression, entrepreneurship, and so on)
- Investments (source of funds, successes, failures, and so on)
- Ambitions and aspirations
- Expected added value to the family and the family business

Ask NextGen family members to complete a personal development plan. This is not meant to put them on the spot, but to help them prepare for the upcoming discussions, and for them to start thinking about their future, independent from the family.

Know Your Family Activity [4]—Memory Lane Activity

Encourage the senior family members to help draw a "family historical chart."

Enlist the younger members of the family to lead this initiative. They are usually great storytellers themselves and can become very creative when it comes to finding information or extracting data from the elders.

The chart below (Figure 1.13) starts in the early 1880s, because most of the patriarchs we have met are directly influenced by that time period. We encourage family trees to represent three to four generations, as each individual is influenced by their parents and the events that influenced their parents when they grew up.

Years	Names	Place of birth	Events in home country	Events in Middle East	World events	Cultural events	Personal events	Successes	Failures
1880									
1881									
1882									
1883									
1884									
1885									
1886									
1887									
...									

Figure 1.13

Prepared collegially, this chart would encourage dialogue and rapprochement among family members. It helps families understand the past and put things in perspective. Seniors would share stories from their youth and walk the family through their storyline.

The family would identify with certain events and would get to better understand the reason why other members behave in a certain way.

Tragedies and other life incidents mark people and define their personalities.

Geopolitical events sometimes create opportunities, but often cause people to take certain life-defining decisions they otherwise would not have taken.

The events around the world over the past century have been greatly influenced by the events in the United States, Europe, the Middle East, and Asia. As a result, people have migrated from one country to another, influencing peoples' behavior, professional orientations, financial status, cultural interests, and so on.

Most importantly, this chart is designed to level the field. More transparency sets in and an open dialogue ensues. It gives family members the opportunity to ask questions and to quiz other members about certain events that would have otherwise remained hidden, or unknown, or even purposely left out, because they were unpleasant or reminded someone of an event they would rather forget or hide, because it may be embarrassing or hurtful, and so on.

Know Your Family Activity [5]—Summarizing the Family History in One Page

Try to identify the most salient events that have marked the family over the years and list them in the chart presented in Figure 1.14.

Use this chart for each family member:

Determining the Social/Political/Cultural/Legal Environment

Year	Family events	Business events	Influencing factors – Social/Political/Cultural/Legal				
			Your country	US	Europe	ASIA	Middle East

Figure 1.14

Know Your Family Activity [6]—What to Do with This Data

Once you have the data, it is important to analyze it and determine how the information impacts the family members either individually or collectively. Items to think about include the following:

- What key events have impacted the family?
- What do you need to know to understand the family dynamics?

- What are the challenges the family is facing/has the family faced?
- Have there been any family tragedies?
- Are there any relationship issues among certain family members?
- Are there any special bonds between some family members?
- Historically speaking, have there been any social or political events that have impacted the family?

Know Your Family Activity [7]—Showcase Family Members

Provide, in one slide, a profile of each family member, including a picture, achievements, education background, extracurricular activities, hobbies, professional undertakings, and so on.

At family gatherings, it would be a good idea to organize sales booths featuring the family business and each of the family member's products and services, especially those undertaken by NextGen family members and in-laws.

Know Your Family Activity [8]—Informal Family Get-togethers

When was the last time the family got together?

Are family gatherings a ritual?

Do family gatherings happen ad hoc, or is there someone who initiates and organizes them?

If the latter, in the absence of this person, who takes over the initiative?

Where do family gatherings take place?

Would anyone among the NextGen family members be interested in leading such an initiative? Family businesses, like all businesses, require leaders who are willing to stick their heads above the parapet. This may be an early indication as to who the future leaders may be.

Know Your Family Activity [9]—Formal Family Meetings/ Assemblies

When was the last time a formal family assembly took place?

What was discussed at such an assembly?

How often do formal family assemblies take place?

Who attends these meetings?

Is there a formal agenda for these meetings?

Who organizes these meetings?

How are the decisions made?

Does anyone take minutes at the meetings?

Are the minutes approved by the attendees?

Who follows up on decisions made and action points from the meeting?

Know Your Family Activity [10]—Family Council/Family Board

Does the family have any representative body (e.g., a family board/ council)?

If yes, who sits on that body?

How are the individuals sitting on that body chosen and appointed?

How often does this body meet?

Who organizes and who presides over these meetings?

What is discussed at these meetings?

How are decisions made?

Does anyone take minutes of the meetings, and who keeps those minutes?

Who follows up on the council's decisions?

Know Your Family Activity [11]—Family Leadership

In the event of a conflict, what happens?

Who is the go-to person?

Is there an appointed family leader?

Do you think it is necessary to appoint a family leader for your family? If yes, what do you think should be the job description of a family leader? What do you think should be the profile/qualifications of a family leader? What is the process for choosing a family leader?

Can an attempt to avoid family conflict actually be the cause of family conflict?

Know Your Family Activity [12]—Family Security

Have you put in place security plans to protect the family members in their home country and when traveling abroad?

Are you monitoring the NextGen profiles on social media?

Too often, careless social media postings by NextGen family members can cause embarrassment to the family (and consequently the family business) in later years when NextGen becomes "the current generation."

Have you put in place programs to coach family members about the need for secrecy/privacy and confidentiality?

Are you monitoring any cyber activities and potential cybercrime activities?

Know Your Family Activity [13]—Contingency Funds

Did you set up bank accounts in secure jurisdictions to cover any expenses the family would incur in cases of medical or other emergency, or force majeure (for example, civil unrest, revolution, kidnapping, and so on)?

Know Your Family Activity [14]—Owners

Who are the owners of the family business?

Distinguish between those who hold financial interests in the business (partners/shareholders), and those who do not (stakeholders).

Know Your Family Activity [15]—NextGen Stakeholders

List who among the NextGen would qualify to become partners/shareholders after the passing of the current partners/shareholders.

Know Your Family Activity [16]—Rights and Obligations

Define the rights and obligations of each of the shareholders and the stakeholders.

Identify the limitations of the rights of each of the shareholders and the stakeholders.

Know Your Family Activity [17]—Exit

Who among the shareholders are looking to exit the family business?

How would you (those remaining) feel if a family member decided to exit the family business?

Have you put in place a mechanism to deal with exits?

Step 3—Know Your Assets

Defining who's who and who owns what is the first step toward separating family matters from business matters.

This step could have been easily called: Know Your Assets and Your Liabilities, and this is the reason why it is one of the most important steps in the succession planning journey, and one of the most controversial.

Sometimes, those in control have difficulty sharing data, while those who are not receiving any data are hungry to receive as much information as they can.

Also, there are cases where those in control do not react well to criticism. In family business, it is often the case that seniors are viewed as heroes. They are not used to systems of checks and balances and consider themselves above being judged by peers, especially younger family members, and those who they perceive to be merely ancillary.

Who Is Transferring What to Whom

Step 3 deals mainly with the *what* part of the equation: The wealth, the tangible and the intangible, core and noncore assets.

As highlighted earlier, it is important to identify what is being transferred in actual terms as opposed to abstract terms. While some of the elements may have been raised earlier, it is important to objectively evaluate and identify what is being passed on/received, to allow family members to decide whether to accept or reject what is being passed on.

One of the fundamental consequences of succession planning is the separation of ownership from management.

Sometimes, the legal structure chosen by the investors dictates the governance structure they would need to adopt.

However, no legal structure will guarantee governance superiority. The tools imposed by law remain subject to interpretation by the people who are called upon to put them to use.

Human nature being what it is, some people will seek to take advantage of the silence of the law and interpret the rules to their advantage, others would seek to be more conservative than they should, and as a result end up choking the business.

The truth lies somewhere in between, and the interested parties would need to strike the right balance, in the interest of the family.

What Step 3 Covers

The *what* in Step 3 includes business assets and non-business assets that are collectively owned by the family (see Figure 1.15).

Business assets
Cash at bank
Shares in core businesses
Shares in noncore businesses
Real estate (land bank, residential, commercial, mixed use)

Non-business assets
Cash at bank
Luxury toys (yachts, private jets, jewellery, artwork, etc. ...)
Leisure real estate property
Private equity portfolio (passive investments)
Philanthropy activities

Figure 1.15

On the Business Side

The nature of the assets, and the objective of the business (what is the business intended to do; market share; profits and losses; short-, medium, and long-term strategy; competition; contingency plans; "black swans" [the bank cashes in on your personal guarantees, your country defaults on its sovereign loan and your access to cash becomes restricted, a global lockdown occurs because of a coronavirus pandemic, etc.]; and so on):

- Legal and tax structures
- Shareholding structures (who owns what, and in which proportions)
- Dividend and reserve policies
- Financing
- Personal guarantees
- Retained earnings (always a controversial subject)
- Leadership
- Management
- Board membership and responsibility
- Family employment

On the Non-business Side

- Personal wealth
- Family home
- Summer home(s)

- Cash in the bank
- Investment portfolios (private equity, assets under management, diversification policy, and so on)
- Banking relationships

Personal high value and luxury possessions (luxury toys) such as private jets, jewelry, car or painting collection, and so on. (ownership, usage, usage rights, maintenance, protection, and so on).

The What

The *what* falls traditionally into two main categories: tangible and intangible.

The intangible assets typically owned by a family in business could be classified as follows:

Among the intangible assets, one may include the family brand name, the family human capital, the family values, and any other intangibles that make up the most valuable assets a family may have.

Also included among the intangible assets, would be the management and leadership of the business. While management and leadership cannot, by definition, be inherited, it is often the case that seniors and founders of a business, whether by tradition or favor, are tempted to pass on the management of the business to their next of kin. This would normally include the leadership role, along with their financial interest in the business.

This represents at least 75 percent of the causes of conflict in a family business. Nepotism often takes precedence over meritocracy, causing more heartache than one may wish to admit.

- Why was X chosen over me?
- I am as qualified, if not more …
- I came into the business first. I should get this job.
- Since we were kids, Dad had a weakness for X over *me*.
- Someone must have influenced his decision … it must be Y …

… are some of the questions that tend to come up.

Defining the Assets

Defining the assets is a *must* conversation.

Sooner or later, the *truth* will come out. The key and related parties might as well be around to explain the facts as they stand.

Once the truth is out, people know where they stand, and they are more prone to forgive and understand. They tend to place themselves in the shoes of the decision-makers and are more tolerant.

It is also an incentive for those who care to get involved and share in the decision-making process.

It is the best way to put an end to the blame game.

- Where were you when we had to make this tough call?
- Where were you when our back was to the wall?
- Where were you when the banks were squeezing us?

... are all questions that come up when senior family members are put on the defensive.

Your Business Is Not Only Your Business

This statement may come as a shock to some.

In fact, your business does not exist in a vacuum.

You may own the financial interests in your business; however, its existence depends on others, including employees, suppliers, bankers, clients, and so on.

All these people are your partners. They have a vested interest in seeing you succeed and survive long term. You are solely the guardian and the fiduciary. They are all watching and monitoring every move.

Today, more than ever before, to be successful in business, transparency, accountability and collaboration are a prerequisite.

It is the new world order we are living in.

The Power of the Name

Family names are for some, an asset, and for others, an identity.

What is a family business without the name behind the business, especially when most world-renowned brands carry the name of their founders?

Disney, Leclerc, Steinberg, Bombardier, Jean-Coutu, Saputo, Hermès, Peugeot, Renault, Toyota, Porsche, Mercedes, Ford, Mars, Krupp, Bauhaus, Armani, Mars, Ferrero, Yves Saint Laurent, Pierre Cardin, and so on.

These are all (brand) names you may know and are likely to recognize.

Some elicit affiliations with products, others with services, and others with cities or countries.

To help you understand the spirit in which this book was written, I would suggest that the next time you purchase a product or a service, or even, visit a city, you look it up, and look up the people behind such products, services, and cities.

Look up the name on the label or the letterhead, and reflect on the people behind such a name, their origins, their history, the environment in which they live and serve, the name of their collaborators, and the values they stand for.

No matter how "corporate" or institutionalized a family business may be, the name behind such a business carries a significant amount of weight. The business is an extension of the person carrying the name and if affixed to a label, the family name, as a brand, essentially serves as a "guarantee," albeit a moral one.

You may recall that in 2010, the group Toyota was brought into public scrutiny after safety recalls regarding acceleration problems with certain models. The Japanese corporate icon had come under threat and its reputation was at severe risk. After some speculation and consumer disquiet, the grandson of the Toyota Founder, Akio Toyoda, held a press conference and stated that he "deeply regretted" the concern that the faults had caused and stated that it was his "personal responsibility" to rectify the problem. Chairman Toyoda also published an announcement where he wrote.

When consumers purchase a Toyota, they are not simply purchasing a car, truck or van. They are placing their trust in our company … as the president of Toyota, I take personal responsibility. That is why I am personally leading the effort to restore trust in our word and in our products.

I find this example quite powerful. It highlights the significance of a family (brand) name, the role it plays, and the responsibility it carries in today's world.

Think about yours and what it represents.

- Who are we?
- What do we represent?
- What if we removed our name from the packaging and replaced it with a generic name?

Know Your Assets Activity

Know Your Assets Activity [1]—List of Assets

In the following box (Figure 1.16), list the tangible and intangible components of the wealth of the family that you believe are being transferred.

Business/Non-Business

Core	Tangible
Non-core	Intangible

Figure 1.16

Know Your Assets Activity [2]—What Value Do You Put On These Assets?

In each of the boxes below (Figure 1.17), list, in descending order, the seven assets you perceive to be most important, and on the corresponding scale, position how important it is perceived by others now and how important you think it will be in the future.

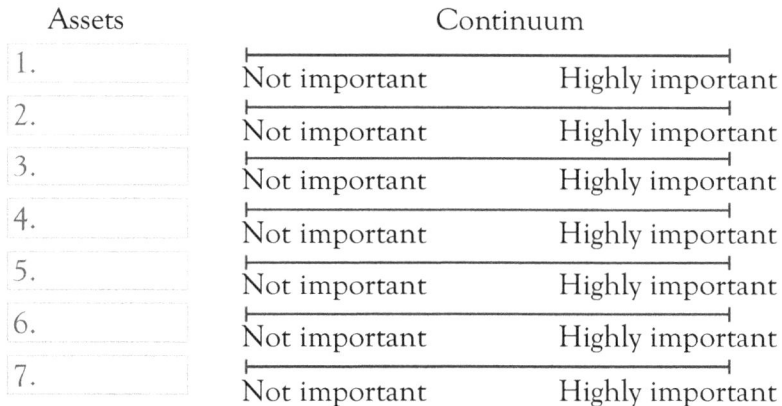

Assets	Continuum
1.	Not important Highly important
2.	Not important Highly important
3.	Not important Highly important
4.	Not important Highly important
5.	Not important Highly important
6.	Not important Highly important
7.	Not important Highly important

Figure 1.17

Having established which assets are being transferred, list, in ascending order, the seven assets you perceive to be most important, and on the corresponding scale, define how important you perceive these assets to be today, and how important you perceive these assets will be 10 years from now.

Know Your Assets Activity [3]—What Do These Assets Mean to You?

Walid's Insights

When dealing with a family business, from a governance angle, it is advisable to keep in mind the separation of ownership from management:

1. *Shareholder proprietary matters (shareholding/financial structure, financing, ownership vs. shareholding, board of directors' role and composition, dividend policy, non-statutory reserves policy, exit strategy, family office funding, family employment, conflict resolution); and*
2. *General corporate affairs (governance, shareholding vs. management, communication and reporting (lateral and vertical), role of CEO vs. chairperson, delegation of authority from the board downward).*

These activities will divide *what* is being transferred into two categories:

- Business-related assets
- Non-business-related assets

This part of the exercise is usually the subject of heated debates. It raises a question: How transparent and forthcoming should these exercises be?

I am of the school of thought that believes these exercises should be as transparent and open as possible.

After you have defined what the business and non-business-related assets are, it is a valuable exercise to ascertain their value for you as individuals and the wider family.

The value that families often place on their assets is that of financial value as well as sentimental value. It is valuable for you to place these assets on the scale depicted in Figure 1.18 to determine the attachment of family members to these assets and the subsequent relationships

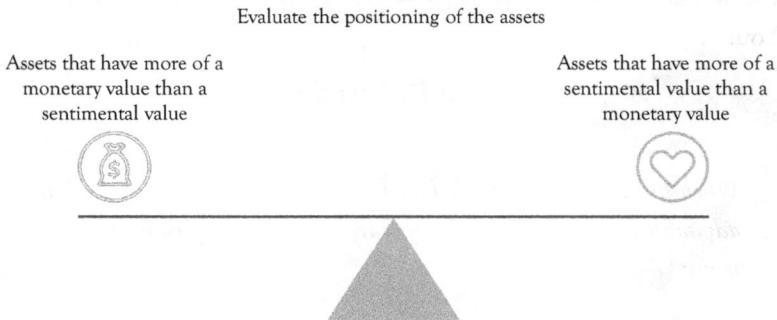

Evaluate the positioning of the assets

Assets that have more of a monetary value than a sentimental value

Assets that have more of a sentimental value than a monetary value

Figure 1.18

Managers of a family business are fiduciaries. They are managing the business on behalf, and in the interest, of other family members. They owe them the truth.

An elder brother who holds the function of CEO is at the service of the shareholders. He is a co-owner and owes his board and his shareholders total transparency. The business is not his alone, and he should not feel he is granted immunity because he is an "elder brother" and/or a "CEO."

He is owed respect, but not immunity.

Also, a patriarch owes it to his siblings and to his NextGen family entrepreneurs to tell them what exactly they are stepping into. They have the right to know *what* exactly it is they are taking over. They need to get the whole picture, with all the details, good and bad.

Any deception, or any perceived deception, will lead to catastrophic consequences, and to major feuds.

Most patriarchs are viewed by their children and grandchildren as heroes. They will earn even more respect if they are forthcoming and share with their next of kin their successes and their failures.

All relationships, even the seemingly strongest, are tenuous. Hiding the truth in a family business will only exacerbate friction within relationships.

Truth has a tendency to surface at some point in time. It is better said by the person who knows it best. There is nothing to be afraid of.

… and let the first one who never made a mistake, cast the first stone.

I: Business-Related Assets

Know Your Assets Activity [4]—Source of Income

What does the family do for a living?

List the businesses the family owns or controls.

Are there any other sources of revenue, other than the family business, that generate a revenue for the family?

Know Your Assets Activity [5]—What Does the Business Consist of

Define the core business.

Define the non-core elements of the business.

Identify the business owned 100 percent by the family, and any part of the business part-owned with others shareholders.

Know Your Assets Activity [6]—Shareholders

List the shareholders (those individuals who own a financial interest in the business) per business activity, per core business, and per non-core business.

Indicate the number (or the percentage) of shares they own.

Know Your Assets Activity [7]—Management

Who manages the family business?

Draw an authority matrix.

Share with the family the *bio* of each key executive.

Identify potential stars among your executives worth investing in, in the long term.

Identify those family members who work in the business.

Share their achievements within the organization.

Share their aspirations for the future.

Share with the family incentive plans and training policies.

Who among the senior managers report directly to the CEO?

How does hierarchy operate in your company?

How lean and how agile is your management?

What is the age pyramid in your company? (How old is the oldest member of management, and how young is the youngest?)

What are the criteria of appointing and selecting senior executives?

How is management remunerated and how are they incentivized?

Do you have an HR policy?

Who is your HR manager?

What are the strengths and weaknesses of the HR manager?

Are there programs for the advancement of the careers of senior management and high-potential employees?

What is your policy for the employment of family members?

Are family members working in the business treated differently than non-family employees?

If yes, why? And if no, why?

Do you make exceptions?

What is your salary policy?

What are your competitors doing in this regard?

Know Your Assets Activity [8]—Corporate Chart

Draw a corporate chart showing the family business as it is organized today, as per the example in Figure 1.19.

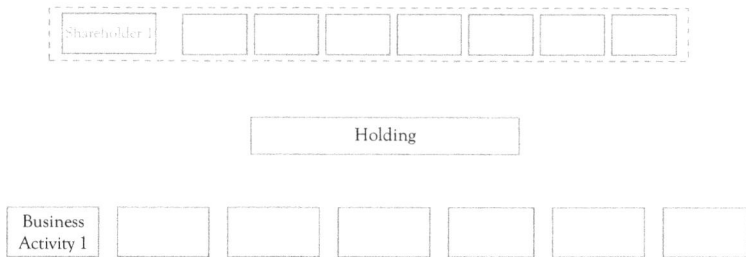

Figure 1.19

Know Your Assets Activity [9]—Decision Making

Who decides *what* in the company?

Know Your Assets Activity [10]—What Do You Know About Your Family Business

What do you know about the business?

Is it successful?

If yes, how successful?

How many employees does it have?

Who leads the company?

Does the company have a board of directors?

If yes, who are the members of the board?

How many are there?

What is their background and professional experience?

What are they asked to do?

Do they receive any remuneration?

If yes, how much?

How many times do they meet within a 12-month period?

How do they make decisions?

Is the board a consultative body, or does it influence the course of business?

Is there a corporate book, where all the resolutions are kept?

Are all the resolutions signed?

Are copies of the agendas discussed kept in the corporate book?

Are copies of minutes of meetings kept in the corporate book?

Who keeps the corporate book with them?

Is there a mechanism that would allow board members to access the corporate book?

Are shareholders or family members allowed to access the corporate book and check its content?

Know Your Assets Activity [11]—CEO

Does your business have a CEO or a General Manager?

If yes, who is this person?

What does he/she do?

What is the CEO's remuneration package?

What do you think a CEO should be doing—his/her job description?

What qualifications should a person have, to be appointed CEO?

What is your opinion of the CEO?

How was the CEO chosen? What criteria were used to appoint the CEO?

Were there other candidates that were shortlisted for the job, and why were they discarded?

Would you like to be appointed CEO?

Why?

Who does the CEO report to?

Does the CEO have any other individuals reporting to them?

Put yourself in the CEO's shoes. What is it you think the CEO does? (See Figure 1.20.)

Do you want to be CEO? Do you think you can do a better job? Why? What makes you eligible for the job?

In their shoes: CEO and shareholders or family members

Figure 1.20

Know Your Assets Activity [12]—Chairmanship

Does your business have a chairperson?

If yes, who is this person?

What does he/she do?

What is the chairperson's remuneration?

What do you think he/she should be doing?

Put yourself in the chairperson's shoes (see Figure 1.21).

What is it you think a chairperson should be doing?

Do you want to be a chairperson?

Do you think you can do a better job? Why?

What makes you eligible for the job?

In their shoes: Chairperson and shareholders or family members

Figure 1.21

Know Your Assets Activity [13]—Financial Status

Does the business have audited accounts?

Who among the family members understands best the financial position of the business?

Who among the family members can explain the financial data?

Share with the rest of the family the assets and the liabilities of the family business, one business activity at a time.

Share with the family successes and failures over the years.

Disclose to the family all personal/corporate guarantees outstanding, and what is the plan to reduce the family's exposure.

Go over each business activity separately, and explain its history, and where it stands today.

Share with the family the future strategy for each business activity.

Share with the family as much data as is available about each business activity the family is engaged in (top 10 clients, top 10 suppliers, competitors, work in progress, cash in the bank, receivables, bad debts, loans, and so on)

Know Your Assets Activity [14]—Risk Management

Are there any geopolitical, legal, fiscal, or regulatory challenges your business is facing, and/or that need to be taken into consideration?

Are there any other risks the shareholders need to be aware of, other than in the ordinary course of doing business?

List all the risks (internal and external) the business has faced over the past five years, and those the business may face over the next five years, and share the plan the management has to mitigate any such risks, per business activity, and for the family business as a whole.

Know Your Assets Activity [15]—Black Swan

Are you prepared to face any black swans? (Plan for the unexpected. A theory more fully developed by Nassim Nicholas Taleb.)

Have you put in place a task force to identify and deal with any black swan that may affect the family business, and as a result the family? Have you contracted any key-person insurance policies?

Have you contracted all the necessary insurance policies covering potential losses your business may incur (foreign exchange, sovereign risk, fire, loss, cybercrime, maritime, and so on)?

Have you made any contingency plans in case of a black swan?

Have you set aside a contingency fund (actual money set aside, and invested in liquid or quasi-liquid products), to cover any unexpected catastrophe?

Know Your Assets Activity [16]—SWOT Analysis

Devise a SWOT analysis of your family business using the format in Figure 1.22:

SWOT Analysis

Strengths	Weaknesses
1.	1.
2.	2.
3.	3.
4.	4.
5.	5.
6.	6.

Opportunities	Threats
1.	1.
2.	2.
3.	3.
4.	4.
5.	5.
6.	6.

Figure 1.22

Know Your Assets Activity [17]—Pressure Points

Define the pressures on the family using the format in Figure 1.23.

	Inside the family	Outside the family
Inside the business	• Family employees • Family shareholders • Rivalry • Ambiguity of roles • • • •	• Employees • Suppliers • • • • •
Outside the business	• Income and inheritance • Family conflicts • • • • •	• Market competition • Political instability • • • • •

Figure 1.23

II: Non-Business-Related Assets

Non-business-related assets are often the cause of latent conflict among family members

Example: One of the heirs, although they would never have raised the matter in family conversation, may be eyeing their father's painting collection or even father's watch, for example, and would feel frustrated if one of their siblings ended up obtaining it. This item may have meant more to that heir for sentimental or historic reasons, but this was never formalized by the deceased. The perceived entitlement may be based on the following examples:

Father told me that when he bought this painting, he thought of me …

Father bought this watch the day I was born, to celebrate my arrival into his world …

Father bought mom this brooch the day I was born …

Know Your Assets Activity [18]—Personal Assets

List the assets the family owns in common that are not the business assets; for example, household effects (china, silver cutlery, furniture, and so on); the patriarch's and matriarch's personal effects (watch, ring, books, personal jewellery, and so on); the patriarch's home, summer home(s), private jet(s), collections of jewellery or artwork or other artefacts, cars, investment portfolio(s), private equity portfolio(s); and so on.

Define the sentimental value, or the monetary value each one of these items have for each family member.

Are there any items a family member is attached to more than any other?

How are personal assets being utilized today?

How do you plan to utilize them long term?

Know Your Assets Activity [19]—Philanthropy

Is the family involved in any philanthropic activity?

Share with the family the details of such activity.

Who among the family members is involved in such activity?

Who among the family members is interested in participating in such activity?

Are there beneficial tax implications by formalizing philanthropic gifts?

Know Your Assets Activity [20]—Administrative Services

Who organizes the family holidays?

Who pays for the holidays?

Who do you call when you need an errand done?

Who do you call when you have plumbing, electricity, or masonry problems at home?

Who do you call when you have an issue with one of your household staff?

Who do you call when you have health issues?

Who do you call when you have a major utility bill to pay?

Know Your Assets Activity [21]—Financial Support

Are there any family members who receive any regular financial support from the patriarch (other than occasional gifts) they wish to continue receiving, following his passing?

Note: Patriarchs or family leaders would be inspired to document any financial support they offer their immediate family, or any member of their extended family, to ensure that such source of income continues in the future. In families where one member is more successful financially than their siblings or parents, we often see such a member contribute complementary monthly salaries, education costs, holidays, or health care expenses, as a gesture of support and love toward those members of their (extended) family, something which is unnecessary and, sometimes, can be condescending. This is a legacy that ought to be carried out by this person's heirs. Sometimes, unfortunately, it is not. A well-documented instruction would help perpetuate the tradition and avoid embarrassment.

Step 4—Know Your Values

In an interview published by the *Financial Times* on October 17, 2018, Ariane de Rothschild is reported as saying:

> *We did a lot of work on values and company culture. On our side there's a panache. Panache is a way of being—it's not vulgar.*
>
> *What I'm trying to build is a bank that is not just a bank. I don't think tomorrow's clients are interested in just a bank.*
>
> *It's very important that my bankers know what wealth is about. I expect more of my bankers than just selling products. Clients want to know more than just the products and I think it's important to share with them our knowledge and philanthropy.*

Values systems are the glue that keeps the family together. In 2020, it is difficult to avoid talking about material matters, about money. It is also difficult to discuss collegiality and collaboration in a world where individualism and self-interest have become the norm.

Family leaders have a gargantuan challenge to keep the family together and to develop and maintain the family fabric.

Behind every successful family business, there is a *hero*.

My great-grandfather is the one who introduced aviation into the country.

My grandfather is the first to have introduced yogurt manufacturing in the region.

My father is the first to have established an orphanage for the underprivileged children in our society.

My grandmother is the first to have established a foundation for battered women in our village.

My grandfather is the one who introduced microfinancing in our country.

We care about the people in our village.

We have a foundation that subsidizes the education of our employees. We pay for this, or that, and so on.

There are many more examples of "heroism," sometimes wrapped up with a sense of nostalgia.

Every family has a story to tell, and every family is proud of its heritage.

It would be good for the family if family pictures and family stories are collated in a book, and if this book is shared with the family members and with the public at large. It should be a source of pride and achievement. It should also be an inspiration for the NextGen and an encouragement for them to take on the mantle.

Every family has a past, a present, and a future.

Yes, grandfather was a *hero*. He did, and did, and did …

Now, grandfather has retired. What are you going to do with his legacy?

Put grandfather aside, for a moment. Now, you are in charge. What do you want to do?

What about *you*?

What do *you* want?

What is it *you* have done to date?

Do you plan to perpetuate your grandfather's memory, or do *you* want to create your own mark?

What do *you* stand for?

What is it you have to show for, and what is it you would like to be remembered for?

Defining the values guiding a family in business is quite a challenging task.

I like to apply the Jim Collins test (see www.jimcollins.com).

1. Why does your business exist beyond just making money?
2. What are your timeless unchanging core values?
3. What are your huge and audacious (but ultimately achievable) aspirations for the future of your group ("BHAGs" for *big hairy audacious goals*)?

In other words:

What would it take to create a "moonshot culture"? By moonshot culture, we mean a future in which many more individuals and organi-

zations are involved in the identification and pursuit of ambitious but achievable goals, in the same way that Bill Gates wants to eradicate polio, Elon Musk wants to "die on Mars, but not on impact," and several start-ups are seeking to develop safe and affordable fusion energy.

—Eric Schmidt and Tom Kalil

[…] If someone has an idea [that] has the potential to make not just sort of marginal or incremental difference, but a really transformative difference, we will try to figure out how Eric and his team can serve as a force multiplier for them.

—Tom Kalil in PENTA, a Burton's Group Publication, December 2019 (www.SchmidtFutures.com)

Answering these questions would bring the conversation to another level and would prove that the family is mature enough to proceed to the next level.

Families for whom values are important appoint a Chief Ethics Officer to act as the guardian of the family values, and to ensure their applicability at both the family and business levels.

Know Your Values Activity

Know Your Values Activity [1]

Consult the family archives and newspapers and conduct interviews with family members and with people who have known your parents and grandparents, and collate those in a book.

You can also go a step further and commission an expert third-party provider (and there are excellent ones out there) to help put together "a family album" or hold the pen while you are telling the family history.

Know Your Values Activity [2]

Collectively, with other family members, try to address the following questions:

- List the set of values that define your family.
- What is the number-one value your family stands for?
- Why does your business exist, beyond just making money?
- What are your timeless, unchanging core values?
- What are your BHAGs for the future of your group?

Know Your Values Activity [3]—What About You?

Does the family name mean anything to you?
Do you relate to the findings about your family so far?
What do you like about it, and what you do not like?
What are you currently doing?
What do you excel at?
Do you care to share what you are doing with the rest of the family?
What do you want to be remembered for after you die?
What do you want to leave behind to your children?
What do you want your children to remember you for?
What about your grandchildren, one day?

Know Your Values Activity [4]—Summary

Defining your vision for the future and developing your succession goals are effective ways to ensure your succession plans are achieved. Your succession vision articulates how you see yourself, your family, and your business in the future.

Goals are measurable targets toward achieving your vision. They should be aligned with, and support your vision.

Succession vision	Succession goals
Reward your employees for their years of support and dedication by ensuring their long-term job security	Pass on the family business to committed and capable owners who would ensure the job security of employees

Figure 1.24

Step 5—Know Yourself

Putting the Individual at the Center of the Family

It is crucial to view each family member on their own merit. Each has a separate legal personality. Each has their own history and trajectory. Each wants to be recognized for their achievements. Each needs to be celebrated individually and as a member of the group.

This is what this chapter is about: people, taken individually, and as members of a group.

- **Who are *you*?**
- **Who do *you* consider to be family?**
- **How do you feel about being part of this family?**

These are three powerful questions. You will be surprised to hear the answer to what appears to be a simple and straightforward question. The answers are usually quite revealing.

Importance of the Question

Now that you have had the chance to know who is who, what is what, and who is transferring what to whom, it is time to look in the mirror and figure out what you really want out of all this. Do you relate to any of it, and do you want to be part of it? And if yes, what price are you willing to pay (that is, the sacrifices, or the compromises, you are willing to make) to remain part of the group?

The reason for all these questions is that each individual has the right to do whatever they feel like doing.

Life is short, and the pursuit of happiness is one's ultimate goal.

Every heir has the right to opt out of an inheritance, and every heir is free to receive their inheritance, and to dispose of it, as they please.

The big question will be: Will I be happier alone, or as part of the group? (See Figure 1.25.)

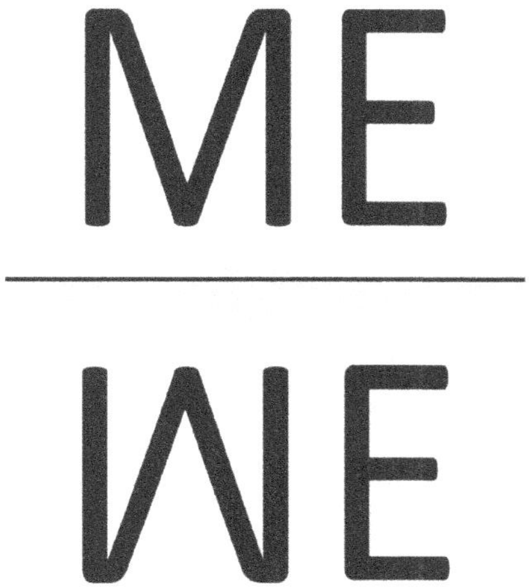

ME

WE

Figure 1.25

The bigger question will be: What would make me happy? Is it money? More money? Or, more of something else?

To pass on an inheritance, or to be the receiver of such an inheritance, will have far-reaching implications for not only the giver and receiver, but also family members and extended family members. An inheritance goes beyond mere monetary value. It will require a 180-degree change in mindset and a great deal of self-analysis before one is ready to accept these challenges. It may be best to study cases of similar life-changing (life-affirming) situations and apply them to how you see yourself in such shoes. Living up to one's heroes is not an easy step. Reading philosophy may help achieve this important goal.

But as some would put it, philosophy will not pay the rent, and will not put food on the table. But other, wiser counsel may suggest that to engage in such a venture with an under-prepared philosophy may lead to rushed and rash decisions in future.

I Want vs. I Need

In order to be able to contribute to the collective mission and purpose, one must be able to clearly define one's wants and needs. As an individual, and a member of a family, one needs to know and be aware of one's deep beliefs, wants and desires, beyond the surface-level awareness.

In understanding one's self, I found that the concept of yin and yang as a metaphor illustrates best the know-yourself exercise. The yin and yang sign symbolizes each one of us as a complete being, having found our perfect balance (see Figure 1.26).

Figure 1.26

Each one of us has been and continues to be influenced by our history, the family we were brought up in, our school, our friends, and the environment we live in and interact with. Our personality and our opinions are forged by a continuous struggle between a series of contradictions, internal and external forces, the good and the bad, the pluses and minuses, and so on.

The ecosystem which an individual is part of or with which the individual interacts contributes to their holistic identity, both cultural and existential. Our cultural identity contributes to our individual ideologies, shared assumptions, and values.

There comes a time when one needs to understand objectively the "me" in them and understand who they are, and how their upbringing and surrounding have contributed to who they are.

Taking it a step further, it is important to delve into your past to explore what made you. History teachers will always preach the mantra that "if you don't know where you have come from, you can't know the correct path to where you are hoping to eventually arrive." Only by such introspection can you confidently go, and can take your family with you.

Ultimately, knowing this information gives you an awareness of who you are and reaffirms your thought process. It is the key to figuring out what you want and (importantly) what the founding members of the family business would expect of you.

This is important because it allows you to understand where your boundaries lie. You will feel better equipped to enter a negotiation and agree to a compromise.

Walid's Insights

You will note that throughout this book there are various exercises that I like to call "me vs. we." These are based on striking a balance between your wants and needs and those of other family members, and the collective majority as a whole.

This is an intrinsic element of the 7-Step Methodology™, as ultimately, once a business passes onto the next generation from one, or from few individuals, to many more, you will be faced with more opinions, thoughts, desires, and ambitions than originally anticipated. The more self-knowledge you possess, the greater the opportunity to stamp your personality on the culture of the business.

The Pursuit of Happiness

While being part of a family business may be rewarding and the right thing to do, it is always important to remember your own pursuit of happiness. This does not necessarily mean that your happiness and involvement in the family business are mutually exclusive, but when you are absorbed in the family business, it is easy to lose sight of your own wants and needs. Therefore, it is important to be proactive in evaluating your position regularly!

Why not make the "pursuit of happiness" one of the objectives of the family, in its family charter?

Know Yourself Activity

Know Yourself Activity [1]

Proactive self-reflection is key to determining your needs and desires. Figure out what you *want* as opposed to what you *need*, in terms of the family business.

Think about what it is that you want and then jot down your thoughts. Below are some questions to guide your thinking:

- What do I associate my self-worth with?
- What makes me happy?
- Who am I?
- What am I working toward?
- What do I want?

Know Yourself Activity [2]

In exploring the "me" in you, it is important to define what it is that you want and what you were working toward in order to fulfill your own ambitions. The table and questions outlined in Figure 1.27 are useful in guiding your thinking.

Focus	Now		In 5 years	
	Description	%		%
Work and business				
Home and family				
Self and personal development				
Community				
Social life				
TOTALS		100%		100%

Figure 1.27

1. Consider how you spend your time now and how you would like to be spending your time in five years. How do you currently invest your time, attention and energy, and how would you like to do so in five years?
2. Note down the percentage of time you currently spend on each of the five potential focus areas (in Figure 1.27), then do the same for how you would like to split your time in five years.
3. Write a few lines to describe how you spend your time now and your aspirations over the next five years.

Know Yourself Activity [3]—Know Your Family/Partner/ Counterpart

List those members of the family who are your partners (shareholders) today.

List those members of the family who can potentially become your partners in the future.

List those members of your own family cell (spouse(s) + children) who can potentially become partners in the family business after you retire or pass away.

Step 6—Know Your Options

Once "me" has been defined, it is important to recognize that within the family business setting, you will be expected to cohabitate with other individuals.

These individuals also have their own view of the way things should be. They may have different wants and needs.

In essence, the yin–yang of one individual must learn to cohabitate with the yin–yang of each one of the other individuals comprising the family (see Figure 1.28).

Figure 1.28

Neither "wants" nor "needs" are necessarily wrong—just different, and to this end, each person can engage in the relationship, and live their life on their own terms.

Walid's Insights

The success of a cohabitation is based on the equilibrium between the following three elements:

- *How me perceives me*
- *How me thinks others perceive me*
- *How in reality others perceive me*

Inspired by the 3-step methodology developed by American sociologist Charles Horton Cooley, "the looking glass self":

1. How do you judge other people?
2. How do you imagine other people judge you, based on how you think these people view you?
3. How do you think of how other people view you, based on how you judge other people?

This section discusses the *me* part of the equation—that is, the role "I" wish to play (or not) as a member of the family business ecosystem.

Walid's Insights

Having explored and understood the "me" and the "we," there comes a time when you have to figure out whether your vision, dreams, and self-purpose are aligned with those of the business, the family, and the stakeholders collectively.

While it is likely that there may not be 100 percent alignment between your aspirations as an individual and those of the business, the family, and the stakeholders, there comes a time when one needs to compromise and determine the extent to which they are willing to make concessions.

Ultimately, the question that poses itself is, do you wish to compromise for the sake of being with others, or would you rather go at it alone?

Because they cannot live on their own, on an island, most people decide to live in a society with others.

They have the choice of making such cohabitation harmonious or on the contrary making sure it is strained.

A harmonious cohabitation would require concessions and effort.

Some succeed in achieving this more than others.

A strained relationship is often due to a lack of alignment.

The same applies within a family.

Early on, each member of the family will be called upon to decide whether they wish to be part of the family business, or whether they prefer to be on their own.

Any successful discussion and any ensuing relationship between two individuals, be it a husband and a wife, two siblings, a father and a son, or even two joint venture partners, are based on the equilibrium between three elements: me, you, and we.

Knowing what I want, knowing what you want, making sure you know what I want and why, making sure I know what you want and why, knowing that *me + you = we*, and that *we* is stronger than the sum of *me + you*, knowing what I am willing to give up to make the *we* a success (the red line *you* should not cross), and knowing what *you* are willing to give up to make the *we* a success (the red line *me* should not cross) is the recipe of success of any discussion and any ensuing durable relationship/partnership (see Figure 1.29).

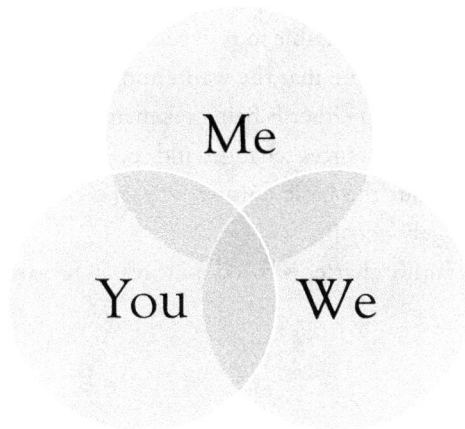

Figure 1.29

This equation needs to be revisited from time to time, to adapt to any changes and developments in the life cycle of either one of *me, you,* or *we.*

There will always be one *me;* however, there may be more than one *you.* The exercise referred to above must apply in the relationship between *me* and every *you.* The end result will be *me* cohabitating with a collection of *you.*

The magic would be to create an atmosphere where each *me* and each *you* find their own internal balance and harmony, in conjunction with that of the family at large.

The Meeting of the Minds

- What do I (*me*) want out of the relationship?
- What do you want out of the relationship?
- Whether we (*me + you* together) is better than me alone and you alone?
- What compromise am I (*me*) willing to make to team up with *you* and form *we*?
- Is the compromise worth it, and for how long?

Compromise in this context is not a weakness but is, indeed, a vital ingredient in the mix to strengthen the foundation of a family in business together. It facilitates a fair agreement where each of the parties feels that their concerns and needs are being met. It will far outlive an agreement where one of the partners feels they have been taken advantage of.

Also, this is why it is advisable to revisit an agreement (family charter), on a regular basis, to ensure that the wants and needs of both parties are still being met, and that neither is being taken advantage of by the other.

Over time, circumstances change and peoples' wants and needs change as a result but the basic culture, if properly and equitably conceived, should largely remain.

A successful family charter is based on three factors (see Figure 1.30):

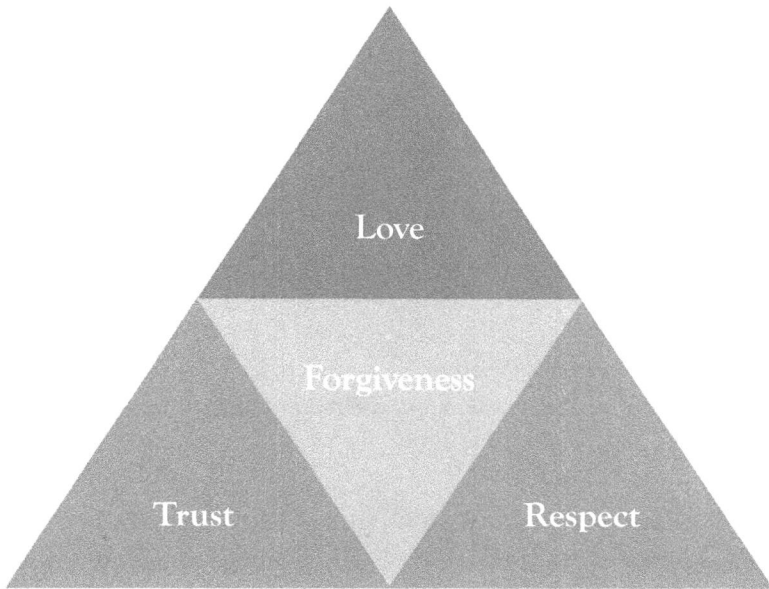

Figure 1.30

Love (and its tandem **forgiveness**) must be continually nurtured. Often it is taken for granted. Like a perfect but fragile flower, if it is not watered on a regular basis, it inevitably dies.

Trust is earned over time. It is built on deeds and words, the matter that makes it vulnerable. It is fragile and highly volatile. It takes sometimes a lifetime to build, but it may be lost in a fraction of a second. One word, or one act, or an omission to act, may destroy the trust that took years to build.

Respect requires maturity and emotional intelligence.

Walid's Insights

Throughout my career as a family business advisor, I have taken on a very forward and direct approach with my families. From the outset I present to them with two options:

Option 1: Staying together

Option 2: Parting ways

Often I am accused of encouraging the destruction of the family business—this is definitely not the case! As I see it, both options are viable. Both options require the most stringent interrogation to ascertain the right course.

What matters is to determine what each family member actually wants.

The answer more often than not is Option 1. What happens next is the determination of the process by which the family will collaborate and cohabitate—all of which will eventually be defined in the family charter.

If Option 2 is the answer, this is still a positive response, because if that is the sentiment and desire of the family, it will inevitably happen whether now, or later (usually upon the departure of the generation transferring the wealth). Where parting is seen to be the best option, it must be done with great care to ensure that the family love and respect is maintained.

Know Your Options Activity

Know Your Options Activity [1]—Me/You/We

What do I (*me*) want out of the relationship?

What do *you* want out of the relationship?

Is *we* (*me* + *you* together) better than *me* alone and *you* alone?

What compromises/sacrifices am I (*me*) willing to make to team up with *you* and form *we*?

Would the compromises/sacrifices be worth it in the long term?

Do I want to give myself time to reflect?

How often do I want to revisit my options? (See Figure 1.31.)

Evaluating the options

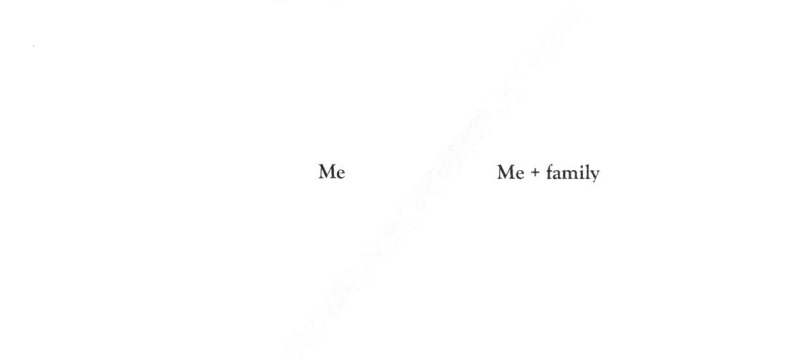

Me   Me + family

Figure 1.31

Know Your Options Activity [2]—Determining Alignment—Vision

Use the tables and tools in Figures 1.32 to 1.35 to evaluate your place in the family business and to determine the extent to which your vision is aligned with the rest of the family members and the family business. Then decide the extent to which you are willing to compromise.

What makes the family unique?

1. What do you think makes the family unique?

❖
❖
❖

2. Why do you think that? Do you have a specific example?

❖
❖
❖

3. What do you think the family business would lose if it was owned by a different group?

❖
❖
❖

Figure 1.32

My definition of success

Figure 1.33

The family business vision

❖
❖
❖
❖
❖
❖
❖
❖
❖

Figure 1.34

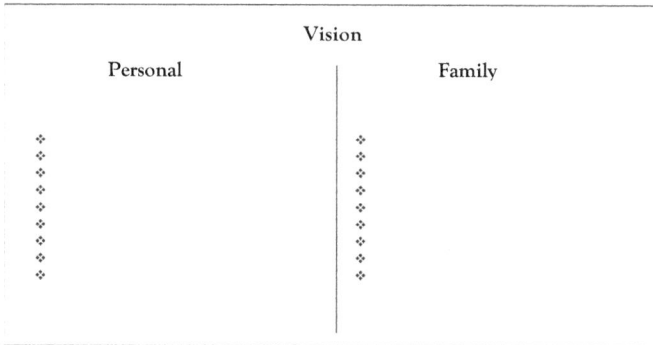

Vision	
Personal	Family
❖	❖
❖	❖
❖	❖
❖	❖
❖	❖
❖	❖
❖	❖
❖	❖
❖	❖

Figure 1.35

Know Your Options Activity [3]—Determining Alignment— Mission

Using the table in Figure 1.36, define your personal mission and compare it to what you believe the mission of the other family members to be.

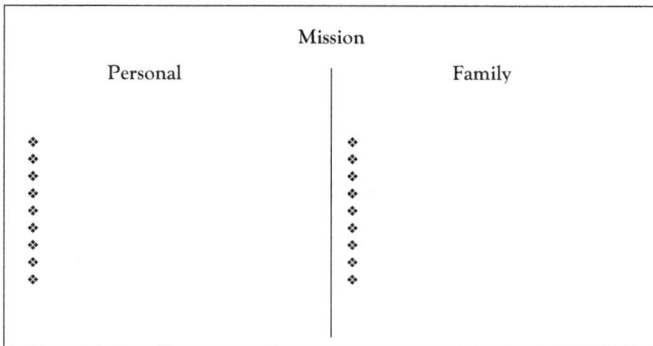

Mission	
Personal	Family
❖	❖
❖	❖
❖	❖
❖	❖
❖	❖
❖	❖
❖	❖
❖	❖
❖	❖

Figure 1.36

Step 7—Know to Conclude

Building and Defining Mission and Purpose

Having gone through the activities under steps 1 to 6, and having decided that *yes, we,* the family will stay together and build a common project, it is time now to conclude.

The three-stage process to reach a conclusion may be summarized as follows:

- Engage *always* in an open and frank dialogue
- Compromise
- Conclude

Engage in an Open and Frank (and Taboo-Free) Dialogue

Communication is the glue that reinforces the bond among all the parties to a family business succession plan.

Establish who's who, and what actually is being transferred. Having determined your *wants* and *needs* and those of your counterparts, it can now be established whether a route forward can be agreed on.

All parties will be invited to establish what needs to be done and decide whether they are willing to uphold their part of the deal.

Compromise

A compromise is essentially an agreement reached by adjusting conflicting or opposing viewpoints, by way of a reciprocal modification of needs and wants.

It is a critical component of any succession planning exercise.

A way to start would be to identify a minimum common denominator, that one element central to the entire equation. This eradicates doubt and allows opposing parties to agree not to disagree. Once this is accomplished, the meaningful conversation can start.

Conclude

While it is essential to "*give time, time*" (François Mitterrand) and allow all family members to express themselves and participate actively in a debate, there comes a time when a debate needs to conclude, and give way to a decision.

This is where a skilled facilitator, or a family leader, can make a difference, if only to help isolate "emotions" and facilitate the discussions between the parties.

Walid's Insights

These activities require an open and transparent conversation among individuals. This may be rendered almost impossible when emotions pollute discussions, for any reason whatsoever.

Further, when emotions are allowed to dominate a conversation, a strange atmosphere sets in, opening the door wide open for miscommunication and distrust. Consequently, conversations will be misinterpreted or misconstrued.

In my experience working with families in business, I find this part of the process to be the most complex to navigate. A family is, by definition, an emotional entity. It is so very important to keep the emotion of family love as the keystone of the business family, but at the same time to remove the same emotion from important decisions in the family business. To do so is to give corporately structured businesses the upper hand in a competitive situation. When skilfully used, the emotional and loving bond of a family in business is the immovable object that stops the progress of the "rolling stone" of the dispassionate corporate entity.

Know to Conclude Activity

This is the ultimate step.

It is the culmination of all that have been said and done throughout the past six steps.

You may have thought that this section may require the most pages. In fact, at this stage, there is not much more an advisor can contribute to the conversation.

This is the much anticipated moment of truth.

You alone are the final decision-maker.

Your life and future happiness depend on the decisions you are about to make.

To paraphrase General De Gaulle, through the activities discussed in Steps 1 to 6 above, you (were) allowed to express yourself freely (from this moment onward); the only thing (you) are not allowed to do is complain.

You are privy to all the information and have had access to all the people who could give you answers. You had your chance to question each step over and over again. Now, it is time to decide. A right mix of the heart and of the brain will be required. Your interests are paramount. You decide. But once you do, you would be required to live with your decision for an uncertain period of time. You are not allowed to rock the boat, as you please. There will be consequences for all your actions, and you will have to pay a penalty if you disrupt the harmony.

Look yourself in the mirror and make a decision. *You* are the only one who knows what lies in the bottom of your heart. You are the only one who knows the "truth," your "truth."

Is it *yes*, I am in, or is it *no*, I am out?

If *yes*, under what conditions?

If *no*, why? What are *my* conditions of exit? (Read about the debate on Brexit. It will help you understand the mechanics.)

Know to Conclude Activity [1]—The Family Balance Sheet

Use the chart in Figure 1.37 to list the pros and cons of joining the family common project.

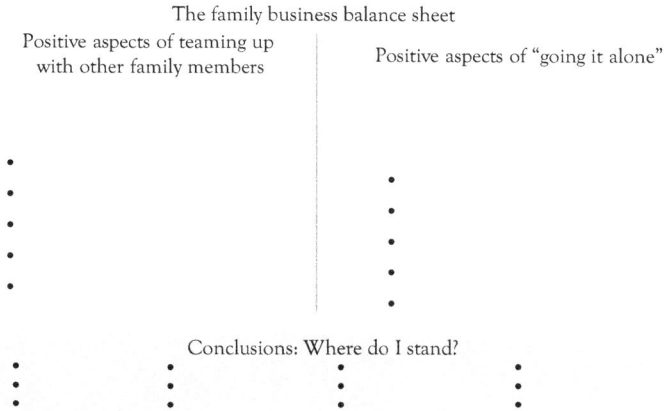

The family business balance sheet

Positive aspects of teaming up with other family members	Positive aspects of "going it alone"
•	
•	•
•	•
•	•
•	•
	•

Conclusions: Where do I stand?

•   •   •   •
•   •   •   •
•   •   •   •

Figure 1.37

Walid's Insights

Differences are bound to arise among the family as individuals—it is imperative that these differences are respected.

It is important to identify and document the key differences and similarities at an early stage. They will serve as the basis of all your discussions going forward. Never assume that the strength of the similarities will negate the power of the differences.

Know to Conclude Activity [2]—Defining the Common Project

Together with the other family members, define what encompasses the common project.

Keep in mind that there are three elements that make up a family business ecosystem: (i) the family, (ii) the family business, and (iii) the family finances.

You would need to address each such element separately and state in simple words how you wish to address each such element and sub- element.

To help you out, consult the checklist in Figures 1.38 to 1.40, and address each point separately.

This will help ease the conversation when discussing the construction of the family charter.

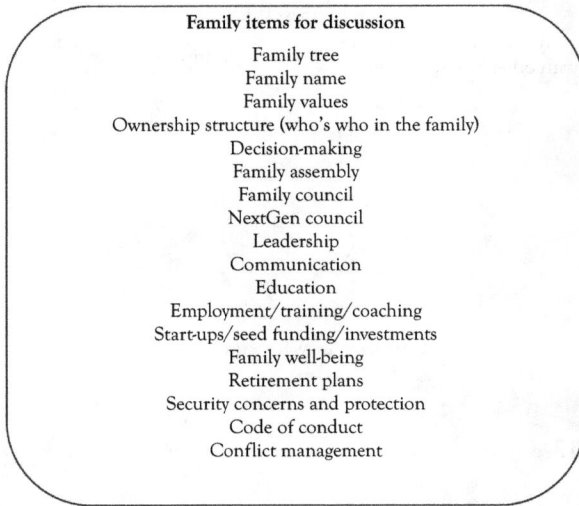

Family items for discussion

Family tree
Family name
Family values
Ownership structure (who's who in the family)
Decision-making
Family assembly
Family council
NextGen council
Leadership
Communication
Education
Employment/training/coaching
Start-ups/seed funding/investments
Family well-being
Retirement plans
Security concerns and protection
Code of conduct
Conflict management

Figure 1.38

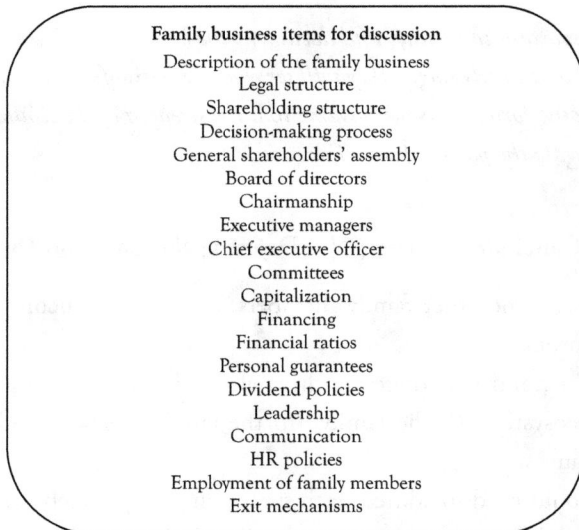

Family business items for discussion

Description of the family business
Legal structure
Shareholding structure
Decision-making process
General shareholders' assembly
Board of directors
Chairmanship
Executive managers
Chief executive officer
Committees
Capitalization
Financing
Financial ratios
Personal guarantees
Dividend policies
Leadership
Communication
HR policies
Employment of family members
Exit mechanisms

Figure 1.39

Family finance items for discussion
Cash deposits
Private homes
Summer homes
Private vehicles
Luxury toys
Investment portfolios
Private equity
Philanthropy
Family well-being
Insurance
Cyber security
Security
Brand name
Administrative services
Concierge services

Figure 1.40

The elements and sub-elements outlined in Figures 1.38 to 1.40 are discussed at length in Chapter III.

Know to Conclude Activity [3]—Six-Circle Model

Use the six-circle model in Figure 1.41 to identify the role or roles you would wish to play as part of the family business ecosystem.

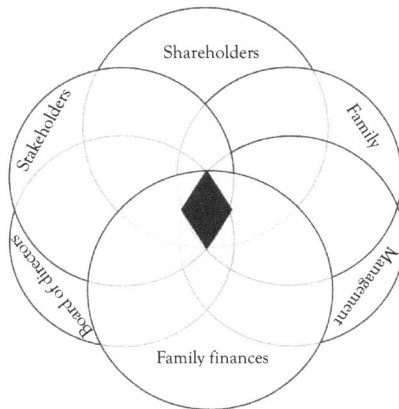

Figure 1.41

Know to Conclude Activity [4]—Setting Expectations: Family First vs. Business First

This exercise is meant to help you define what you are willing to invest into the business, and what you expect to get in return.

Ask not what your country can do for you, ask what you can do for your country.

—John F. Kennedy

What President Kennedy said may easily be rephrased to replace "country" with "family business." In other words, what is it you expect to get out of the family business, and what should the family business expect to get from you?

Do you wish the business to grow so that it can support all the needs of the family, or do you wish the family to sacrifice its well-being to ensure that the business grows and continues to thrive? Or do you envisage something in the middle: grow the business and ensure the family is well taken care of? (See Figure 1.42.)

This is the conversation that would need to take place at this stage. It is all about setting expectations.

Defining priorities
What is the common goal?

Striking a balance

Family first   Business first

Figure 1.42

Not all family members have the same financial capabilities and thus purchasing power. Some are richer than others, and some have better-paying jobs than others.

Each family member has certain needs they wish to fulfill. Should they look at the family business as their teller machine that should satisfy and bankroll all their needs, or should they look at the profit they generate from the family business as a "complementary source of income," "a kind of bonus" they would receive if and when the business is doing well?

Setting expectations and managing those expectations are essential should a family wish to establish and maintain a healthy, peaceful, and productive relationship.

As a family, it is important to determine where you fall in terms of your expectations.

Individually, and as a family, answer the multiple-choice questions below, circling your choice:

1. Shareholders should receive annual fixed dividends to maintain their lifestyle regardless of the financial performance of the business:
   Yes No
2. Those family members who do not work in the business should receive monthly/yearly payments from the business:
   Yes No
3. Family members employed in the business should receive higher compensation in the business than other employees:
   Yes No
4. Employment of family members in the business should be a birthright:
   Yes No
5. The CEO position/and other top leadership positions in the business should at all times be held by a family member regardless of their qualifications and experience:
   Yes No
6. The business should bear the expenses of family members:
   Yes No
7. The board of directors should be composed of family members as opposed to independent directors and should prioritize family member candidates as opposed to others:
   Yes No

If you have answered "yes" to the majority of these questions, it indicates a "family first" culture as opposed to a "business first" one, and vice versa. This is not necessarily a bad thing; however, it is relevant to know that it is essential to establish the appropriate business governance structure to support the family's culture.

I usually give the following example to help family members decide the course of action:

Pretend for a moment that your business is a farm. You own 100 cows that produce 700 gallons of milk every day.

If, at the end of the day, all the milk produced is given to the owners of the farm to drink and to dispose of, what do you think will happen over time?

If, on the contrary, part of the milk is kept at the farm, and the balance is distributed to the owners, then the farm would be able to sell the milk it has in its possession, or produce cheese and butter with it to generate revenue, feed the cows, and eventually breed and grow its herd, to generate more revenue and grow the business.

Indeed, what may feed five shareholders today, may not be enough to feed 10 tomorrow, or 50 in a few years.

The same applies to a business.

Go back to the questions above and apply the same reasoning as with the farm and the cows.

Did your answers change?

Would you prefer that the business distributes all the revenue it generates to the shareholders, or would you prefer that the business and the shareholders come to an agreement as to how much should be distributed to the shareholders and how much should be kept with the business? (See Figure 1.43.)

Succession planning: Where giving and taking meet
What may be enough to feed a family of two, may not be enough to feed a family of four.

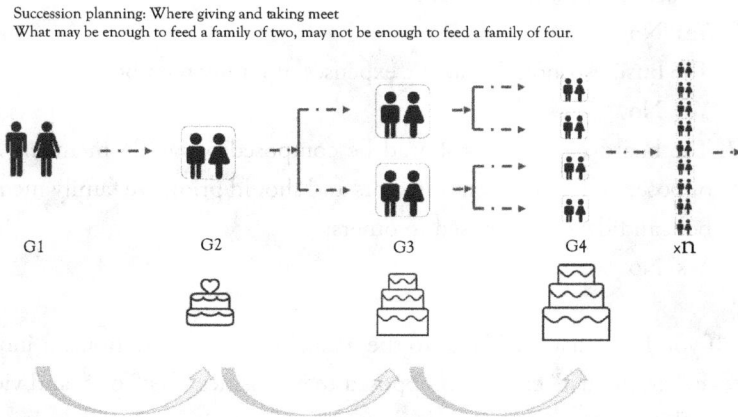

Figure 1.43

CHAPTER II

Succession Plan Conditions of Success: The Hard Work

The fault, dear Brutus, is not in our stars, but in ourselves, that we are underlings.

—William Shakespeare, Julius Caesar

To Ace It … You Need to Face It

Experience has shown that a succession planning journey is hard, long, and tedious.

To ensure success, it is expected that all parties concerned, seniors and juniors, play their part and pull their weight.

As mentioned earlier, in family business, what you see is not necessarily what you get. Decades-old skeletons tend to surface when least expected, and historical baggage, assumed to have been discarded, tends to find its way surreptitiously into otherwise peaceful and structured conversations.

It is for these reasons that families engaged in a succession planning journey should be willing to work relentlessly, to unearth the "truth" (the real facts behind the smiles). They should deal with it in a mature manner—with *intelligence*, open mind, and open heart.

If names be not correct, language is not in accordance with the truth of things. If language be not in accordance with the truth of things, affairs cannot be carried on to success.

—Confucius

To earn success, they need to deserve success.

In other words: *to ace it*, they need to *face it*. (See Figure 1.44.)

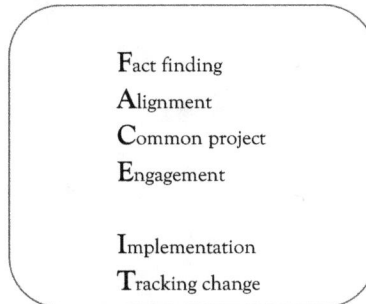

Fact finding

Alignment

Common project

Engagement

Implementation

Tracking change

Figure 1.44

The six stages that would make the journey successful may be summarized as follows:

Fact finding refers to:

1. Identifying *all* the elements characterizing a given business family
2. Understanding each such element, and its overall influence
3. Questioning the status quo and unearthing the "truth"

Alignment refers to family members engaging in an open and no-holds-barred dialogue leading to a decision to stay together (or not) and to engage in a common project together (or not). They must establish the rules of engagement by which they are willing to abide to ensure the success of this common project, its stability, security, and long-term sustainability.

Common project refers to the partnership among the family members who wish to build something together, summarized in a written instrument, commonly referred to as the family charter. In this, the family members illustrate their future together in detail, and document the agreed rules of engagement. Signing the family charter seals their commitment.

Engagement refers to the buy-in and the active participation of *all* family members, seniors and juniors alike, and to their commitment to the success of the exercise.

Implementation refers to the phase following the signature of a family charter. It will stress-test the family to determine the stability, security, and sustainability (3S's) of the family charter, at the three levels: the family, the family business, and the family finances.

Tracking change refers to the monitoring and the review mechanism the family will establish, and will apply, to assess the progress of implementing the family charter and ensure that the rules of engagement they concurred remain valid and fit-for-purpose.

Our Approach

This book covers the first three stages defined above:

Fact Finding will put the family business in perspective. It will define the concepts and explain our approach to family business succession planning, mostly based on deconstructing the facts and of challenging the status quo.

Alignment will go to the heart of the subject and will discuss consensus building using our seven-step succession planning methodology. It is the precondition to devising a workable and sustainable family charter.

Common Project will discuss in detail the construction of a family charter and the various components it comprises. Sample select provisions of a family charter will follow.

Chapter II discusses what I mean by *Fact Finding, Alignment,* and *Common Project,* which were discussed at length in Chapter I, and are the basis for Steps 1 to 7.

As for Engagement, Implementation, and Tracking Change, they would need to be tailored to meet with the requirements of a given family. This book only addresses the approach and methodology.

Fact Finding

The fact-finding exercise is intended to put things into perspective and help define what it is we are really dealing with when we talk about family business and related succession planning.

This section is divided into three subsections, as follows:

1. Putting the Family at the Center
   (a) Defining Family Business
   (b) A Matter of National Security
   (c) The Elements Comprising a Family Business Ecosystem
2. Faux-Amis: Calling Things By Their Name
3. The Art of Deconstructing

1. Putting the Family at the Center

Over the past few years, the term "family business" has taken center stage and has become the buzz-word of self-proclaimed professionals in the legal, business, financial, banking, fiduciary, and academic worlds.

But what is a family business and what does this term refer to?

(a) Defining Family Business

There are as many definitions of the term "family business" as there are family-owned/-controlled businesses in the world.

There is, however, a consensus among scholars and professionals to refer to a business as a family business when the said business is owned or controlled by a family. Rarely are new businesses founded as a family business. Rarely will you hear someone say: I am setting up a business with the intention that my children take over from me once I retire or I am dead. People usually start a business either to pursue a dream or a passion, or to build something and make a living.

In general, a business qualifies as a family business in two cases: (1) the founder(s) passed away or retired and the business has already passed to a second generation of owners and/or managers, or (2) it has been set up by one or more individuals and is in the process of being transferred to one or more of their children.

To *own*, in this context, refers to the financial interest a person may have in a given business—in other words, the shares that person may own in the capital stock of a company. Later in this book we will discuss the difference between "ownership" and "shareholding."

To *control* is used herein in a legal context. In most jurisdictions it refers to the individuals who (1) own more than 50 percent of the financial interests in a legal entity and/or (2) have enough influence to appoint the managers and the directors of a company, or to steer the management decisions of a company in a certain way.

While the definition of *family* has evolved over the years, depending on the social environment people live in, in most countries, it is still used in the traditional sense. It refers, in general, to a family cell comprising one father, one or several wives, and the children born to each of the wives. While polygamy is outlawed in the Western Hemisphere, it is still an accepted social phenomenon in some countries in the Middle East. It gives rise sometimes to complex family structures.

A family business is not limited to a car dealership, a manufacturing plant, or a mom-and-pop shop. It could also refer to a real estate portfolio, a financial institution, like a bank or an investment house, or any other business activity owned and/or controlled in common by a sibling or a cousin consortium.

Family businesses represent the majority of private companies (as opposed to government-owned), whether partially listed on a stock market or not.

(b) A Matter of National Security

Family businesses across the world represent the backbone of most economies. They represent between 65 and 90 percent of the private sector, depending on the country where they operate.

In most cases, they are the largest employers and contribute large portions to the gross domestic product (GDP) and tax revenues in most of the countries where they operate.

A new world order is taking shape before our own eyes. It is shaking up the foundations of the economy as we know it, hanging the vulnerable out to dry.

We predict that in such an unstable environment, only those family businesses that have instituted and introduced sustainable governance rules and procedures would have a better-than-even chance of survival.

In many parts of the world, the sustainability of family businesses has become a matter of national security.

A Call to Arms

I will not go as far as calling for a family business-type Marshall Plan; however, I would like to appeal to governments and to central banks across the world to create an environment that sustains existing family businesses, encourages "non-business" families to use their combined strength of will and purpose to create family businesses, and to actively promote succession planning at family-controlled businesses as a risk management tool.

At the same time, I would like to appeal to families in business to give succession planning serious thought, as the businesses they own are not theirs in perpetuity. They are mere guardians of these businesses and, as such, they owe a fiduciary duty to their stakeholders and to society at large to keep these businesses afloat and to help grow them.

Finally, I would like to appeal to the *hobbyists*, those self-proclaimed family business advisors, who read a book or two on the subject matter, and pretend they understand family business. I urge them to stay away and to refrain from offering sterile solutions for the sake of making a buck. You are doing these families more harm than good, and you are making our job more complicated.

(c) The Elements Comprising a Family Business Ecosystem

Family-owned and/or-controlled businesses do not operate in a vacuum.

They are part of a complex ecosystem comprising a number of systems and subsystems. Taken separately, these are autonomous and contradictory in nature, but the survival of each depends, to a great extent, on their interaction with one another.

When you work closely with families in business, you discover that their world revolves around three elements, as follows (see Figure 1.45):

1. The family—that is, the people behind the business;
3. The family business—that is, the business activity the family, as a group, is involved in; and
4. The family finances—that is, the assets and the money the family owns, other than the family business.

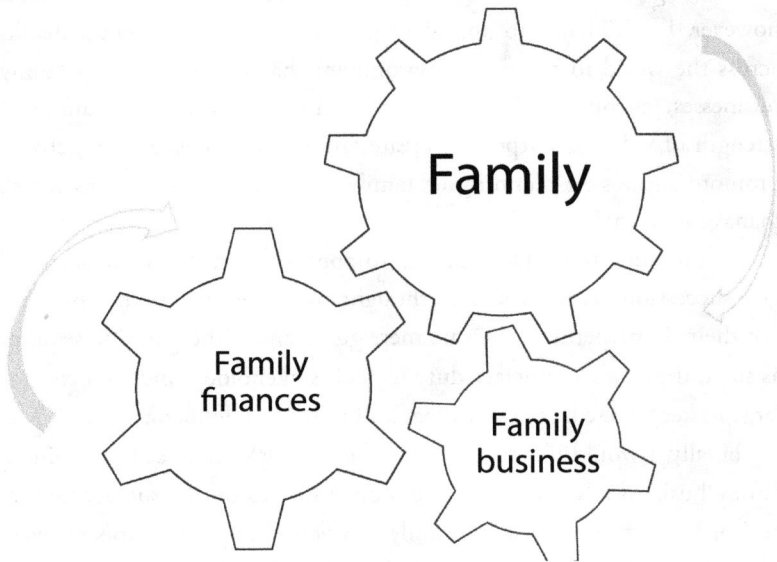

Figure 1.45

Each element has its own life cycle. Each evolves at its own pace, and none are static.

Family comprises more than one individual. The life of each starts at birth and ends with death. The first time I told a patriarch that one day he will die, he paused, then looked at me with wide-open eyes, and said:

"You know, you are the only one who told me I was going to die one day. None of the people who surround me ever dared tell me this. Yes, you are right, it is time to do something before it becomes too late."

It is not a matter of "if" but of "when." Unfortunately, no one controls this part of the equation.

Between birth and death, many things happen. Each one of us has their own story to tell.

A business concern is the same. One never knows where a business adventure may take you. Every business has its ups and downs, and every business develops and grows differently.

The same principle applies to financial wealth. There is always the first dollar you earned or inherited. From there on, you are the master of your own fate. You can spend it, save it, or grow it.

These three elements evolve in parallel but remain intertwined. Any development at the level of one of them, be it positive or negative, has the capacity to influence the evolution of the other two.

Looking closely at each such element, one would note that they differ fundamentally.

While family matters are mostly intangible, based on emotions and on private and conflicting interests, family business matters and family financial matters are mostly tangible and based on rules and regulations, some of which are volatile and market driven. Others are regimented, and legally construed and corporately constrained.

As a result, no universal "best practice" governance rules apply to family businesses and no "one-size-fits-all" family charters can be imposed on families in business.

Each family business is unique and each of its elements is unique and autonomous and should be treated as such. Each is driven by its own energy and each abides by its own protocols or governance standards. In this book, we will refer to these standards as follows: family governance, corporate governance, and financial governance.

The success of a succession planning journey is dependent upon (1) understanding the dynamics between these three types of governance rules, (2) respecting their differences, and (3) striking the right equilibrium between them, in the interest of the family and that of the family business.

Our Philosophy

Our work has reinforced the belief that, irrespective of how sophisticated and financially prudent any legal, accounting and tax structure may be, family businesses remain fragile and will not survive in the hands of NextGen family business entrepreneurs unless the core family matters are addressed to the satisfaction of *all* family members.

> We have observed that many professionals focus on the business side of the equation and discard the family side, protesting that family matters are private and should not be the concern of management experts.

On the face of it, such an approach may be legitimate.

However, in a family business context, one cannot limit oneself to dealing with one aspect of the equation (business) and ignore the other aspects (family and money) especially if this other aspect is most influential and has the power to destroy everything that is being built, with one word or gesture. Those engaged in a family enterprise should ask themselves what the core values are for which our family is known and respected. This can be of greater value than the most sophisticated (and therefore expensive) marketing campaign and an element that can never be reproduced by the corporately structured business (see Figure 1.46).

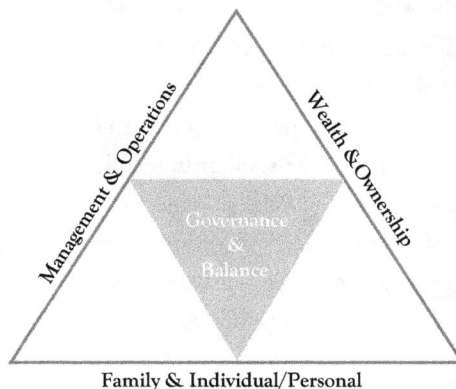

Family & Individual/Personal

Figure 1.46

It is common to receive a request from a family in business asking for a governance framework for its business.

It is rare, however, to hear a family say:

We have spent a substantial amount of time discussing among ourselves a vision and a plan for the future. Now that we know what we want, and where we are headed, we would like you to help us devise a governance framework for our business.

To the novice, these two requests may be the same.

A governance framework for a family business differs from a corporate governance manual.

A family business governance framework does include a corporate governance manual, but it also includes more.

One can download a corporate governance manual from the internet. You will note that most look alike, although some are more customized to fit the circumstances of a particular business than others. They will, however, all have similar content.

For many, the language used may sound alien to them. This is simply because corporate governance rules and regulations are mostly dictated by company laws prevailing in a given jurisdiction.

Modus Operandi

I refer to corporate governance and shareholder manuals as the *modus operandi*. They define the way a corporate entity operates. They set out the rights and obligations of "shareholders" (that is, the holders of financial interests), the manner in which a company is managed, and the manner in which profits and losses are disposed of.

A corporate governance manual, however, will not deal with matters relating to the relationship among family members, the manner in which a founder will relinquish power and retire from active duty, the manner in which they will pass on the baton to a NextGen family leader, or the manner in which siblings will carve out the world among them, their relationship with the community, their long-term vision, and their values system. In other words—the family company ethos.

Excuses, Excuses …

We have seen multiple examples in which seniors, or siblings holding senior positions in a family business, face "family unrest," "turbulence," or "questioning." The response is often to commission, at great expense, major corporate governance reforms, simply to divert the attention of those they perceive to be "ungrateful rebels" or "mutineers."

They do so to avoid, or to delay, dealing with the underlying and sometimes "embarrassing" questions.

What they do not realize is that ignoring their base and not showing leadership will lead to loss of trust and to more turbulence, and eventually to conflict.

It is almost always beneficial to "bite the bullet," so to speak, to address the issues that perturb the family, to instill peace and harmony among the stakeholders.

People who carry responsibilities are fiduciaries, and are accountable to others.

Modus Vivendi

In a family business context, "others" may include an elderly mother who has never seen a balance sheet in her life, a cousin who is eight years old, or a brother who lives 10,000 miles away and has never set foot in the family business. Regardless, they are all "shareholders," "co-owners," and stakeholders.

They need to be recognized as such and be respected accordingly.

"Humoring" them, and reporting to them, comes with the job.

I refer to the rules that govern the relationship among the members of a family in business as *modus vivendi*. They refer to all the matters a corporate governance manual will not. They refer to matters the law has not addressed, leaving it instead to the discretion of the people behind the business. They ensure harmony within a family business context and, as much as possible, seek to reduce, if not eliminate, any risk of slippage when managing a conflict. They protect the special bond and ethos of a family business.

Conflicts are part of human nature and are inevitable. In a family business context, they should not be suppressed, but every effort should be made to resolve them with understanding and judicious wisdom. This is the true test of leadership in this scenario. One needs to try and prevent, if not preempt, conflicts, and manage them adequately when they occur.

This subject will be discussed in more detail in later pages.

It is true that the term "family business" comprises two words: family and business.

However, family + business do not necessarily = family business.

While we place family at the center of any business succession exercise, we also address each of the other two elements that make up the family business equation: the family business and the family finances. This being said, we do put more emphasis on the family and on family matters, knowing very well that, if we miss a step, all the work we do on the "business" and the "finances" sides will fall apart, at the first opportunity a crisis hits the family or the business.

Three factors underpin this philosophy:

- Human nature
- Money and the effect it has on people
- The ever-evolving values system

(a) Human Nature

Despite what you hear, or believe in, human beings are not born equal. Some are born with a silver spoon in their mouth, others not. Some are healthier than others. Some are smarter. Some are prettier. Some are wittier, and so on.

Jealousy, envy, hatred, and rivalry cohabitate with love, affection, and camaraderie.

Psychology and psychiatry teach us that these are traits that exist in every single one of us, and even between parents and children, among siblings, and among cousins.

The manner in which people behave with one another is not the subject of this book.

We only need to highlight that these traits exist and that they affect people's behavior and relationships with one another, and they cannot be ignored.

In a family business, the family needs to identify these traits and take note of them. If left unattended, they have a tendency to fester and poison the relationships among its members. Sooner or later, they will surface and cause irreparable damage. There is no sense in hiding behind one's finger, and pretending that they do not exist.

Conflict erodes trust.

The cycle of conflict may be summarized as outlined in Figure 1.47.

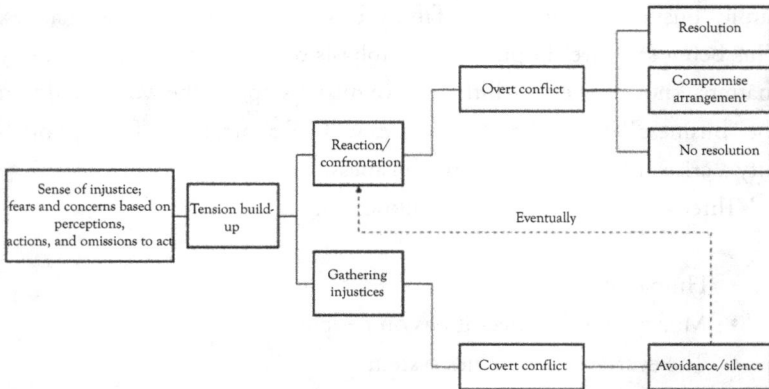

Figure 1.47

(b) Money

Many of the families in business I have worked with are families with financial wealth.

I have observed that the relationship people have with money is very personal. Certain relationships are healthier than others.

In many cases, money is a corrupting factor. For some people, money is an end, but for others, it is a means to an end.

Many among our NextGen family members had difficulty dealing with money and many among the seniors had difficulty teaching their children the value of money and the way it should be managed.

For some, money seemingly grows on trees; for others, it takes sweat and blood to generate, and is dear to them.

This disconnect between generations often cohabitating under the same roof has, in many cases, caused dramas within families.

For many who feel entitled, "the bottom line is the dollar sign." Nothing else counts.

The money factor alone, if not addressed properly in a family business succession planning context, will distort the outcome of any exercise.

Discussing money in public is deemed to be, in certain circles, taboo and depends very much on the cultural context.

People may be happy bringing up the subject in private, but not in public.

Unfortunately, "money makes the world go around," as the song goes, and in 9 out of 10 of the mandates we have worked on, money has been the main underlying subject that no one is willing to bring to the table. It is like the elephant in the room that no one dares address directly.

"Father does not give me enough."

"I am taken for granted. I am not paid a fair wage."

"I need so much to make ends meet."

"Why is my sister-in-law better off than me?"

"Why is the non-family CEO earning more than me?"

"Look at my brother's house, and how he is living. Why not me?"

"Father loves my sister more than me. He keeps on buying her stuff."

"My husband always brings a gift for his mother when he comes back from a trip, not me."

"Our inheritance is blocked because my brother is selfish. He has money, I don't."

"My elder brother always lectures me about my spending habits. Who does he think he is?"

"My father died, and my uncles no longer give us the same income he used to bring home."

These are but a few of the examples we hear as we gather data.

(c) Values Systems

The world in 2020 has nothing to do with the world in 1920, or 1820.

Globalization and artificial intelligence have disrupted societies to their core.

A new generation of highly educated boys and girls are hitting the market. "GenZees" (Generation Z, those born after 1996) and the Millennials before them, are challenging the status quo and are demanding to sit at the table with the big boys—and to be heard.

This has resulted in a shake-up in the value system governing the relationship among people for centuries.

At the *family* level: the *pater familias*, as it was known for generations, has disappeared. Parents (can) no longer "whip" their children into shape, and primogeniture, as has been practiced for centuries is being challenged, as more educated women enter the workforce.

The concept of parenthood is changing, and the role of parents is evolving.

The spotlight is now on the role of "education" (at school) + "upbringing" (at home) + "general knowledge" (personal development), and the manner in which they shape people's behavior and attitude.

At the *business* level: Slavery has disappeared and the master–servant relationship has evolved and is gradually being replaced with a more collaborative employer–employee relationship based on trust and mutual respect.

NextGen employed in the family business are no longer taken for granted and are now competing alongside non-family member employees and executives for positions and promotions.

Nepotism is fading away and is being replaced by meritocracy at all levels. Siblings and cousins (current or future shareholders) are watching, and they now have a voice.

In today's world, privacy is compromised. Transparency has become the norm.

Faux-Amis: Calling Things by Their Name

Over time, certain words and expressions have made their way to the family business literature, causing some confusion among authors and families.

In this book, the following terms shall have the meaning ascribed below:

1. *Business Families*

Business families are those families who manage and/or *control* and/or own the majority financial interest in a given business. The term *families in business* will be used interchangeably.

2. *Governance*

The term *governance* refers in general to systems and processes that are meant to help better manage and govern a given body. In a family business context, one tends to distinguish between "governance for family business" and "financial governance."

Governance for family business deals with governance at the level of the three elements that make up a family business: the family, the family business, and the private/financial assets.

As a result, we tend to distinguish between three distinct types of governance: family governance, corporate governance, and financial governance. Each such term is used in a specific context.

In a corporate environment, one expects that governance introduces transparency and empowerment, and with that, accountability and responsibility.

In a family business context, one expects, in addition to the above, that governance results in the separation of family matters from corporate matters, and emotions from reason. One further expects better communication, more fairness, and more inclusion.

Family governance refers to the rules that govern the relationship among the members of the family behind a business, and the relationship of the family with that business (often the source of the financial wealth) and with the assets owned and purchased with the money generated from the business (the *modus vivendi* among family members.)

Corporate governance refers to the rules that govern the operation of the business and the relationship between the owners of the business, its managers, and other stakeholders (the *modus operandi* of the business.)

Financial governance refers to the rules that govern the management of the assets, other than the business assets, that are owned collectively by the family members.

3.   *Institutionalization*

Institutionalization is the term used when families in business separate ownership from management while favoring meritocracy over pure nepotism. In other words, when they introduce structures and protect those structures with rules (systems and policies) that (i) apply to all without distinction (where no one individual is above any said rules), and (ii) ensure the business is managed by the most competent individuals, irrespective of whether said individuals are family members or not.

Institutionalization is also about separating ownership from shareholding, emotion from reason, mind from matter, the conscious from the unconscious, and the spiritual from the physical.

> *Idea meritocracy—i.e., a system that brings together smart, independent thinkers and has them productively disagree to come up with the best possible collective thinking and resolve their disagreements in a believability-weighted way—will outperform any other decisionmaking system.*
>
> —Ray Dalio, in *Principles*

4.   *Next Generation (NextGen)*

Next generation family business entrepreneurs refer to those boys and girls who will be taking over from their seniors the control of a given family business. They are the future. They are the enablers of tomorrow.

5.   *Shareholders vs. Owners*

In a family business context, I tend to distinguish between *shareholders* and *owners*.

In a legal context, *shareholders* are those individuals who hold a financial interest in a property, be it a legal entity or a real estate asset. In some countries, the term shares are loosely used to refer to the financial interests one owns in a limited liability company (LLC). As a general rule, no shares are issued when forming an LLC. The financial interest owned by a partner in an LLC is referred to as "parts" or simply "financial interests." In a legal context, the term "shares" is used if the company being established is a corporation (or joint stock company [JSC], or Société Anonyme), with shareholders owning the shares in the capital stock of the corporation.

Most of the literature uses the term "owners" to refer to family members who have a financial interest in a family business. I prefer however, to distinguish between shareholders, owners, and stakeholders.

Distinguishing between these three categories of individuals steers the conversation away from the "business" and instead focuses on the "family," and goes to the heart of succession planning.

For me, *owners* are those individuals who have a sense of belonging. They are the ones whose legacy, name, or brand is attached to the business, and who care more about the long-term gains than the short-term profits.

The *stakeholders* are those individuals who interact with the business, and who have a stake in its success, other than the shareholders or the owner. The term includes, without limitation, employees and third-party service providers, such as bankers, auditors, suppliers ... also family members working in the business.

This book will take into account those individuals who hold more than one function—that is, those individuals who are employees, and who are also shareholders, and/or family members, and will deal with their status accordingly.

6.   *Process vs. Journey*

The literature and most consultancy firms tend to use the term *process* to describe the steps required to complete a succession planning exercise. I prefer to use the term *journey*.

A process *implies* a rigid timeline associated with certain deliverables. I am not convinced that the term *process* may be applied to family business succession planning, as it is incompatible with the nature of the subject matter we are dealing with. My approach to succession planning is family centric, as opposed to business centric, and when dealing with a family, you are dealing with human beings who have emotions and are capable of reason (heart vs. brain). My work, in a nutshell, is based on finding the right equilibrium between these two elements.

For this reason, my preference is to use the term *journey*. As with a process, a journey has a beginning and an end; however, it is more flexible, in the sense that it can be modulated and adapted to account for any emotional outbreaks or expressions along the way.

A process is by nature rigid. A journey is on the other hand more elastic. When applied to succession planning, it grows organically at the pace of the slowest member of the family. Deliverables remain at all times a function of the needs of the family.

7.   *Succession Planning vs. Estate Planning*

The terms *succession planning* and *estate planning* have been used interchangeably in recent literature. In fact, they relate to two different things.

Succession planning relates to the act of passing the baton from one generation to another. In a family business context, it deals with the transfer of wealth from one generation to another. This concept is discussed at length in this book.

As for *estate planning,* it is a legal concept. It refers to planning one's inheritance to avoid or preempt any confusion or misunderstanding and, sometimes, feuds, among heirs.

The Art of Deconstructing

When you first meet a family, they tend to overwhelm you with facts.

To make sense of what is being thrown at you, you need to take a step back and try to understand.

Our role, as advisors, is to identify all the facts and investigate the "who," "what," "why," "when," and "how."

We "deconstruct." We kind of reverse engineer, and dig deep to unearth the "truth." Once we have all the components we need, we then "reconstruct" and draw a clear picture.

I like to compare family business advisory to artisanship.

A family business advisor ought to approach a mandate like a horologist, or a watch repairperson, would.

There is a mix of science and art in designing and building a watch and later, in repairing it and making sure it works and gives the time in an accurate fashion, day in and day out.

The same principle applies when devising and implementing a family business succession plan.

What do you think a watch repairperson will do when you bring a watch to them and say: "I don't know what's wrong, my watch no longer keeps the time, or my watch has stopped working, or …?"

After examining the watch with their bare eyes, and from all angles, the first thing a watch repairperson would typically do is to take off the back cover and use one of those tiny magnifiers to check the inside of the watch.

After a thorough examination, they would proceed to take the watch apart.

They would remove all the pieces in the watch, one by one, clean them, and examine them.

They would repair or replace the defective pieces, and reassemble the watch.

They will then test to see if what they have done solved the problem.

If yes, they will call you and ask you to come and pick up your watch.

If no, they will start the process again, and again, until the watch is repaired.

They would "deconstruct" the watch, and would "reconstruct" it again.

Did you know, that on average, a modern watch has between 250 and 350 pieces, and that it takes the patience of an angel to deconstruct and reconstruct a watch, sometimes several times, until it is properly repaired?

You are going to tell me that some watches are sometimes beyond repair. In this case, the only thing to do is to take stock of this fact and decide what to do: either wear the watch as jewelry, knowing that it is useless and will never give you the time, or put it aside (put it in a drawer, display it in a vitrine at home, or donate it to a museum) and replace it with a new, modern version. It still works on the same principle but implements more modern science and technology to perfect its purpose.

The same applies in matters of succession planning. There are cases where the members of a family do not see eye to eye, and are not willing to compromise or agree on a common project.

The decision will come down to: Do we salvage the relationship among the family members or do we sacrifice the family for the sake of making money, or more money? Or do we employ up-to-date methods to diminish the parts on which an agreement is floundering and rebuild a new structure where the family culture is safeguarded?

Decisions of this sort require courage, wisdom, and determination.

They are made after having gathered all the facts and investigated all the alternatives.

Some are harder to take than others, but taking the right decision requires the decision-maker to put aside any emotional considerations and use reason instead.

I use the same approach when facilitating a family business succession journey.

Deconstruction

I start every mandate with a fact-finding mission.

It is the first and the most critical phase of the entire succession planning journey.

Doctors will call this exercise diagnostic. Trial lawyers will call it discovery, and mergers and acquisition (M&A) professionals, due diligence.

I tend to call it "continuity audit."

Continuity refers to the initial intention for introducing a succession planning exercise and to a family's desire to continue together the journey their seniors have started. A succession plan refers to a plan that lays out the steps that would allow someone to "succeed," or to take over something from someone else, in an orderly fashion and "continue" the journey that someone has started.

What would be the purpose of the exercise if the person who will take over does not continue the work of their predecessor?

Families who seek our help are those who are looking to find out: (1) what is out there and what has been done so far; (2) is it worth anything, and is it worth passing on; (3) are there any takers out there; and (4) if the answer is yes to (2) and (3), then who, and how.

Audit refers to the facts as they are made available on a given date, and to the fact that all the underlying elements have been identified and checked.

Taking over someone else's business is no simple task.

It is a decision that is at the same time rational and emotional. It involves the heart and the brain, and striking a balance between the two is quite challenging. Stepping into someone else's shoes would require the parties to know and understand all the elements that make up such business, understand the pluses and minuses, and get into it confidently and with the optimism of a full knowledge of the task ahead.

As mentioned earlier, rare are the families who look at governance as preemptive medicine.

Businesspeople are usually absorbed by their day-to-day tasks, and many prefer to postpone the inevitable until the inevitable happens.

Sometimes destiny will play bad tricks on people.

Unfortunately, none of us knows the date, time, or circumstances of our death, leaving behind a parent, a sibling, a spouse, or a child who will be called upon to deal with "our mess."

This is a fact of life.

Death is part of life, and we cannot escape it.

This is something families in business, seniors and juniors alike, need to keep in mind and act upon. This is especially true when they are at the helm of an important business and have responsibility for a great deal of wealth.

Preventive medicine has proven to be more efficient, and in the long term, a cheaper option than curative medicine, especially when a latent issue develops into a crisis.

"I don't know anything about the business."

"My father (husband) never discussed business at home."

"I never knew the business had so much debt."

"I never knew Dad had issued so many personal guarantees. What if … we go bankrupt?"

"Who is this person on my father's right-hand side? He seems to control my father."

"Why tell us this now? What is he hiding?"

"What is my sister doing at the factory?"

"Why is my brother on the cover of this prestigious businesspeople 's magazine?"

"Why does he get all these invitations to attend fancy parties, and not us?"

"Why does he take his son to all these business meetings?"

"He flies first class … in a private jet. Who pays for this?"

"My brother is always on a plane."

"I don't even know what we own."

"Every time I ask for money, I am told the business is not doing well. Yet, my brother drives a Ferrari."

"To start with, what is my brother doing there? I thought this company is my father's."

"I am an owner; I can do whatever I want."

"Every time I ask the accountant to show me balance sheets, he finds an excuse to send me off. Next morning I get scolded by my brother. Who does he think he is?"

These are all examples of what we hear when we first meet a family.

Like with the pieces of a watch, a continuity audit would help identify all the elements of the family business ecosystem, and would lay them down in a logical and systematic manner.

A place for everything, and everything in its place.

—Benjamin Franklin

Continuity audits are conducted by asking relevant questions, challenging the knowns and the unknowns, and processing the information as it becomes available.

Reports that say that something hasn't happened are always interesting to me, because as we know, there are known knowns; there are things we know we know. We also know there are known unknowns; that is to say we know there are some things we do not know. But there are also unknown unknowns—the ones we don't know we don't know. And if one looks throughout the history of our country and other free countries, it is the latter category that tends to be the difficult ones.

—Donald Rumsfeld

We dig as deep as we need to until we are able to unearth (what I call) the "truth," that is, all the relevant facts that are useful and that are relevant to help the family build a comprehensive and sustainable common project.

While in many cases it takes a family several months, if not several years, before it decides to embark on a succession planning journey, I found that once the family makes up its mind, and once it chooses "the advisor" who is going to accompany it through this journey, masks fall, and tongues loosen.

As the journey progresses, people open up and share details that are of interest to them.

Sometimes, one needs to tread carefully. In most families, emotions tend to run high, and many people get offended very easily, if put in an uncomfortable position.

The role of advisors is to inspire confidence, and to encourage their interlocutors to speak freely.

We remain neutral. We do not judge, and we do not make any comments.

Meeting every family member and spending the time necessary to put them at ease is a delicate task. It requires dexterity, tact, and diplomacy.

Gathering information is a long-term endeavor. It is like repairing a watch. If you miss a step, or if you miss a piece, the watch that has been entrusted to you will never work properly. You keep on searching and you keep on digging until you find a breakthrough. It could be that a previous unscrupulous watch repairperson removed inadvertently a piece and never replaced it, or as is sometimes common with rare pieces, non-professionals would borrow from one watch to repair another, or it could be that the piece you are looking for simply fell under the desk when you dismantled the watch.

No matter what the reason may be, you keep on searching until you find the missing piece(s), or you find an alternative solution. But under no circumstance would you give up, or compromise your integrity, or the well-being of the person who entrusted you with what may turn out to be the most valuable thing they have.

This is additional proof that succession planning is not a process. It does not fall within pre-set parameters.

Dealing with fellow human beings is always gratifying. I always come out of a continuity audit exercise a better overall and more empathetic person.

It is a strange feeling when people confide in you and share with you their most intimate secrets. It is even more humbling when the people who confide in you make you feel that somehow their happiness and that of their family depends greatly on the outcome of the work you are doing.

Fact finding is like going on an adventure.

All you know is that you are embarking on something new, but you don't know what to expect, and what the ultimate outcome will be.

Mind you, some adventures are more fun than others.

Inevitably, seniors will start by saying that all is good under the sun, and that they invited you in either because they wish to retire sometime soon, and it is their desire to make sure that their succession will take place in an orderly fashion, or because someone in the family has been making noise, for some time, about something insignificant, and they felt it was perhaps time to invite a neutral third party to investigate and make the issue go away.

"We called you because our bankers told us we have to organize" … "Family X told us that you have done some work for them, and they like you"

... "We went to a seminar ..." "I read a book, and I think it would be beneficial for the others to understand what it means to introduce governance...."

Otherwise, "there is no problem, or conflict on the horizon." "We are a happy family." "We all love one another." "We all have respect for one another." "We have a board, I am the Chairman, all decisions are taken in harmony" ... "I started the business, I gave my brothers a share, they do as I tell them. They are happy ...."

"But ... since you are at it, please tell my son" ... "tell my sister" .... "tell my brother" ... "tell my father" ... "they keep on asking questions, or enquiring about this or that, or questioning my decision to do this or that ...."

There are cases where continuity audits are overwhelming.

Often, family members will try to enlist you as their spokesperson. Others will try to trick you into siding with them against other members. Some are more insecure and apprehensive than others. You will be watched continuously, and your loyalty will be constantly tested.

No matter what, advisors need to remain neutral and remain, at all times, at an equidistance from every member of the family.

Looking Through the Magnifier

It is easy for someone to visualize a watch repairperson dismantling the pieces of a watch. Most of us have seen it done, at least once in our lifetime.

What about a family business? How would you go about dismantling its pieces and figuring out what's what, and who's who?

We mentioned above that the family business ecosystem comprises three elements:

- The family
- The family business
- The family finances

Each one of these elements comprises a multitude of sub-elements.

The literature refers to them as systems and subsystems, respectively, because each such element and sub-element is powered by a certain energy and can be interpreted in many ways, thus affecting the ecosystem they are part of (see Figure 1.48).

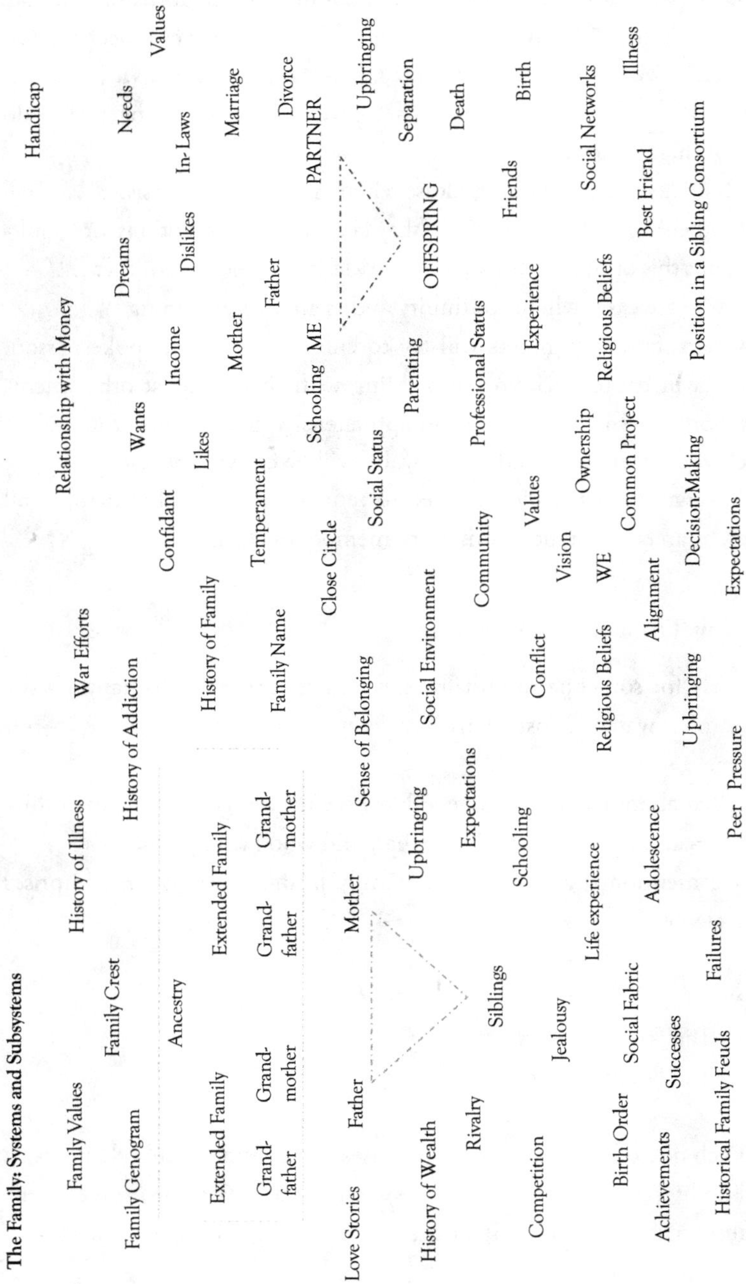

The Family: Systems and Subsystems

Handicap
Values
Needs
Upbringing
Relationship with Money
In-Laws
Marriage
Separation
Dreams
Divorce
Birth
Wants
Dislikes
PARTNER
Death
Income
Confidant
Mother
Father
Social Networks
Likes
ME
OFFSPRING
Friends
Temperament
Schooling
Experience
Illness
War Efforts
Parenting
Religious Beliefs
History of Family
Social Status
Professional Status
Best Friend
History of Addiction
Family Name
Close Circle
Community
Ownership
Position in a Sibling Consortium
History of Illness
Extended Family
Sense of Belonging
Social Environment
Values
Common Project
Family Crest
Grand-mother
Conflict
Vision
Ancestry
Grand-father
Upbringing
WE
Decision-Making
Family Values
Extended Family
Expectations
Religious Beliefs
Alignment
Family Genogram
Grand-father
Grand-mother
Mother
Schooling
Life experience
Upbringing
Siblings
Adolescence
Love Stories
Father
Social Fabric
Expectations
History of Wealth
Rivalry
Jealousy
Birth Order
Successes
Peer Pressure
Competition
Achievements
Failures
Historical Family Feuds

Figure 1.48

Looking through the magnifier, a *family system* may look like this.

The sub-elements represented in Figure 1.48 are not exhaustive.

If taken separately, each such sub-element represents a world by itself.

They will differ from one individual to another, as each family member would have a different life experience and would react and interact with such elements and sub-elements in a different manner.

The same would apply within a *family business system* (see Figure 1.49).

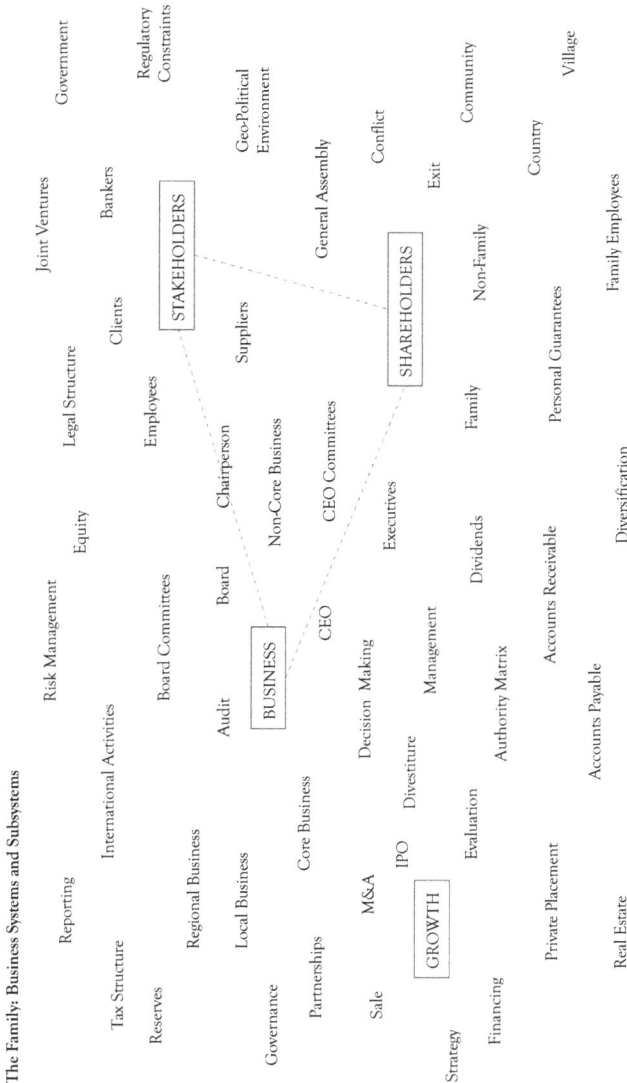

The Family: Business Systems and Subsystems

Figure 1.49

While the sub-elements that make up a family business system may be less complex than those comprising a family system, they remain equally as important.

A business system is mainly driven by commercial, legal, financial, accounting, and banking considerations. Most are regulated and are subject to rules that have been tried and tested over the years.

It remains, however, that the management relies on human interaction, the same as family.

It is the human element that spoils the broth and distorts what would otherwise be a pure science.

Alan Greenspan, the then-Chairman of the US Federal Reserve Board, coined the term "irrational exuberance" when referring to the overheated dot-com bubble in the 1990s. Later, in the aftermath of the 2008 crisis, "experts" invented the concept of "emotional intelligence and investor behavior" to justify why analysts, rating agencies, and central banks missed the signals that led to one of the most severe recessions to date.

They blamed it on "human behavior" and on "irrational reactions."

Looking at a *family business system* with a magnifier, one would see something similar to what is shown in Figure 1.49 above.

Again, this picture may not capture *all* the sub-elements, or subsystems of a business system; however, it shows the complexity of the subjects that need to be taken into consideration and analyzed, prior to issuing any prognosis.

The same applies when you look at a *family finances system* with a magnifier (see Figure 1.50).

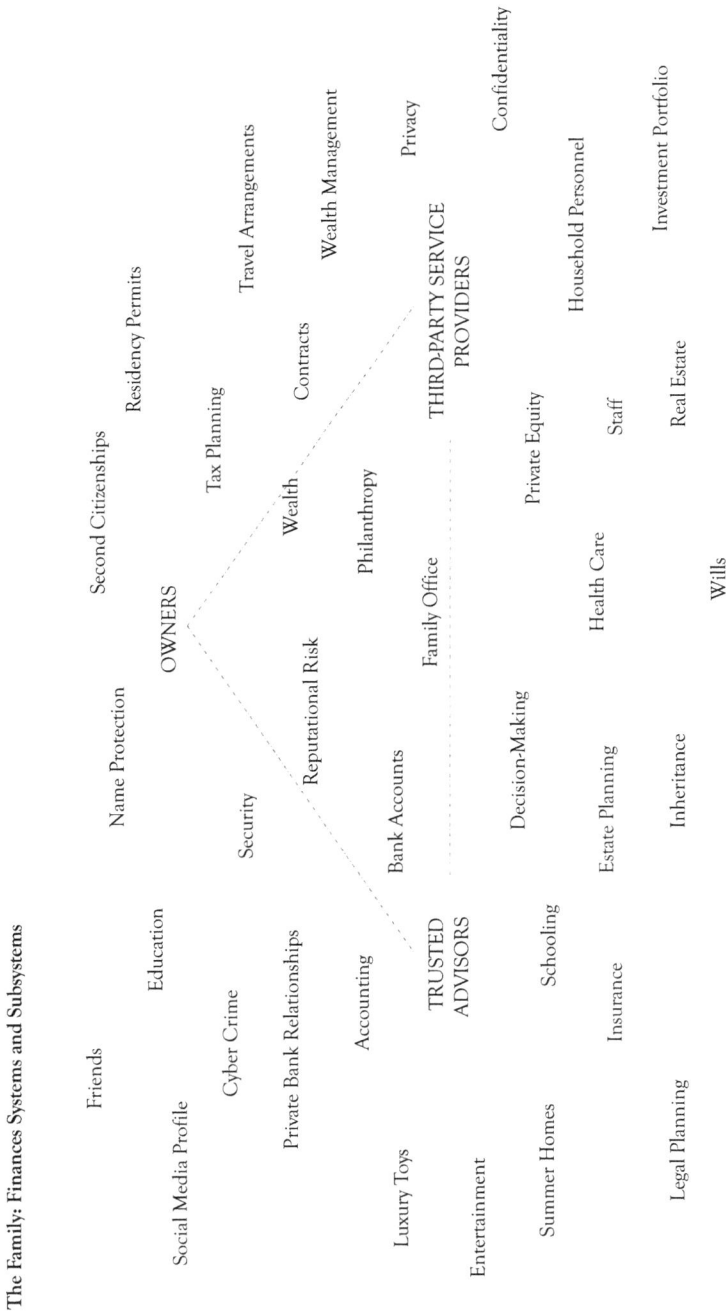

The Family: Finances Systems and Subsystems

Confidentiality

Travel Arrangements

Privacy

Residency Permits

Wealth Management

Investment Portfolio

Second Citizenships

Contracts

THIRD-PARTY SERVICE
PROVIDERS

Tax Planning

Household Personnel

Name Protection

Wealth

Philanthropy

Private Equity

Real Estate

OWNERS

Family Office

Staff

Reputational Risk

Health Care

Security

Wills

Bank Accounts

Decision-Making

Education

Cyber Crime

Estate Planning

Inheritance

Private Bank Relationships

Schooling

Accounting

TRUSTED
ADVISORS

Friends

Insurance

Social Media Profile

Luxury Toys

Summer Homes

Entertainment

Legal Planning

Figure 1.50

Most analysts dismiss the role money plays in the relationship among members of a family in business, and most fail to realize that money, singlehandedly, can make or break a relationship among siblings or cousins.

Family finance systems may be compared to a Trojan horse. You can see it, but you can easily miss the surprises it may hold. Once the gates open up, you may be faced with the biggest surprise of your life.

Managing expectations is an art, and predicting the improbable, is a science. (See: *The Black Swan: The Impact of the Highly Improbable*, by Nassim Taleb.)

Data Processing

Once we identify all the elements and sub-elements defining a given family business ecosystem, we proceed like the watch repairperson would.

We analyze each element separately, and each element in conjunction with each of the other elements and sub-elements that make up the family business ecosystem.

This exercise is multidimensional in nature. It needs to be conducted at three levels simultaneously, as follows:

- At the level of each individual member of the family
- At the level of the family, as a group
- At the level of the family at a given time in its life cycle, and within the environment it is living in, at that given time

As a result, we end up with an indefinite number of combinations and triangulations.

Managing Combinations and Triangulations

Helping a family devise a 100-year roadmap is a challenging task. Keeping an even keel and maintaining an equidistance from every family member is equally as challenging.

A facilitator is the keeper of the family secrets and holds in their experienced hands the future well-being of a family in business. They steer the ship that holds the family treasure through dangerous waters to where it can do the most good for everyone in the family.

As such, it is very important for a facilitator to understand the elements they are dealing with, and master the ensuing triangulations.

Each family business element has its own governance parameters. They differ in nature, but nevertheless must *in fine* cohabitate in a harmonious manner, in the interest of the family and that of the family business.

When looking at the figures above, which represent the *family systems*, the *family business systems*, and the *family finances system*, you may have noticed that certain words or expressions were linked together, forming a triangle (see Figure 1.51).

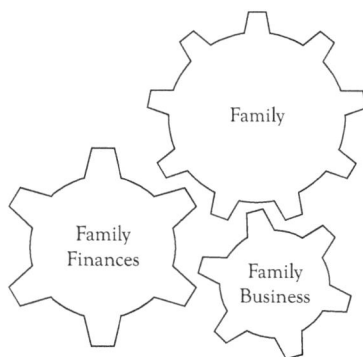

Figure 1.51

The reason for this is that each system and subsystem is governed by a number of rules (I call them governance rules) that are specific to that system and which need to be addressed adequately.

Referring to the definitions given above, *family governance* focuses on the rules governing the interaction between the following three elements:

- The dynamics among the family members themselves
- The relationship between the family members and the family business
- The relationship between the family members and the family finances—that is, the (a) money and (b) source of money

Corporate governance focuses on the rules governing the interaction between the following three parties (see Figure 1.52):

Figure 1.52

- Shareholders—that is, those individuals (family members or otherwise) who own a financial interest in the family business
- Managers of the family business (whether board members, executives, or employees); and
- Stakeholders (other than the shareholders and the managers, who are affected directly or indirectly by the well-being of the family business; for example, suppliers, bankers, joint venture partners, clients, the country/province/village where the business is located, and so on).

Financial governance focuses on the interaction among the following three parties (see Figure 1.53):

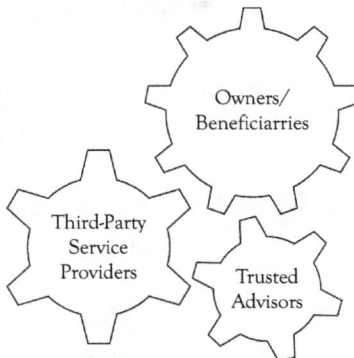

Figure 1.53

- Owners of the family finances
- Trusted advisors, who manage the family finances
- Third-party service providers

Identifying a Minimum Common Denominator

Deconstruction helps level the field and helps put the parties on the same wavelength.

Once the challenges a family is facing are clarified, and once the broad outline of what needs to be done (the big picture) is acknowledged, we proceed with identifying the lowest common denominator among the family members, as a prerequisite to defining a roadmap that will be the foundation to constructing a durable and sustainable family charter.

Very much like a watch repairperson.

The next phase is to put the pieces back together and start reconstruction.

(Re)Construction

This phase is akin to Henri Kissinger's famous "step-by-step" diplomacy.

It requires the facilitator to engage in one-on-one discussions with each member of the family, and, where appropriate, conduct group meetings and facilitate the dialogue among family members, without betraying any of them, and maintaining total neutrality and independence vis-à-vis the process.

Alignment is about (re)construction.

Engage, engage, engage, and then conclude.

—Christine Lagarde

Throughout this process, the *coup d'œil* and the individual touch (*tour de main*) of the family business advisors will bring them closer to being an artisan.

Conclusion

This section was designed to introduce family business succession planning and show the complexity of the endeavor a family embarks on when it decides to engage in such an exercise.

It is also meant to show that a succession planning exercise is not a mere process. Rather, it is a journey, which starts early in the life of every family member. It is multidimensional and multicultural by nature. No one standard fits all, and no best practice can be imported into a family in business. It evolves organically, at the pace of the slowest family member.

Every time you feel the urge to give up or to go faster, think of Albert Einstein and his theory about the time it would take him to save the world.

Indeed, each family is unique, and the experience is personal to each family member.

The role of a family business advisor is that of a facilitator. They ask the hard questions, stir the pot, and are expected to bring some order to the chaos they unravel.

A family business advisor is no magician, though. Some situations are broken and are beyond repair. Sometimes it is too late to salvage the wreckage. It is unfortunate—but it is not the end of the world.

One can still pick up the pieces, and with some humility and hard work, can rebuild.

Humans are attracted by success. Family members in a family business context are the same.

In the midst of the worst storm, a leader can bring calm and make the whole difference.

Don't look at the advisor for the solutions, look within. Identify that leader, empower them, and follow their path.

An advisor can only help dissipate the dust created by chaos, and help you see the path ahead more clearly.

The advisor is not the solution. The family is.

Family members need to live with their choices and seek happiness and fulfillment.

The Glue That Ensures the Stability, Security, and Sustainability of the Family Business: Communication

Communication, Communication, Communication

If you have an important point to make, don't try to be subtle or clever. Use a pile driver. Hit the point once. Then come back and hit it again. Then hit it a third time—a tremendous whack.

—Winston Churchill

"Communication" is to succession planning what "location" is to real estate.

It is the uncomprising ingredient that ensures the continuity and the sustainability of the family business in the hands of the NextGen.

It helps make the family business world go 'round. It increases the level of trust, and instills harmony in the relationship among family members.

Indeed, trust and respect are the two ingredients responsible for maintaining a secure peace in what is otherwise a situation prone to failure.

The strength of a family business is based on the strength of the relationship among the family members behind the business. The more united they are, the stronger their business.

Throughout the history of the genre, family businesses have faced innumerable challenges. The people behind the business would need to rely on their leaders to help them navigate through the storm. And the only way they can trust their leaders, in today's world, is to engage in a periodic and structured communication (see Figure 1.54).

Listening respectfully to, and acknowledging the needs, the wants, the fears, and the expectations of others is the essence of communication.

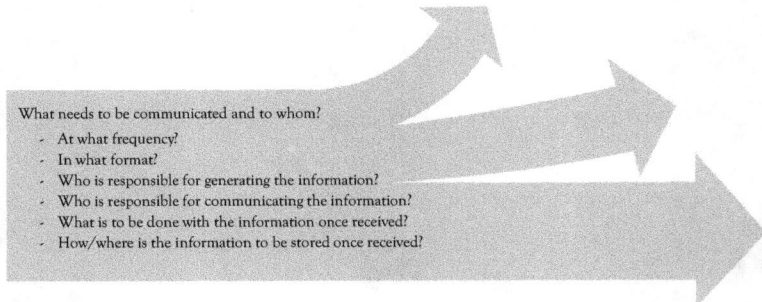

(Responsible) Transparency and Managing Expectations

What needs to be communicated and to whom?
- At what frequency?
- In what format?
- Who is responsible for generating the information?
- Who is responsible for communicating the information?
- What is to be done with the information once received?
- How/where is the information to be stored once received?

Figure 1.54

Structures and rules assist in the orderly transfer of information to and from.

Having separated the two worlds (family from family business), it becomes imperative to define the rules of communication and interaction between the various players at both levels, the family and the business, and the interaction between them.

Figure 1.55 illustrates the channels of communication typically employed within a family business.

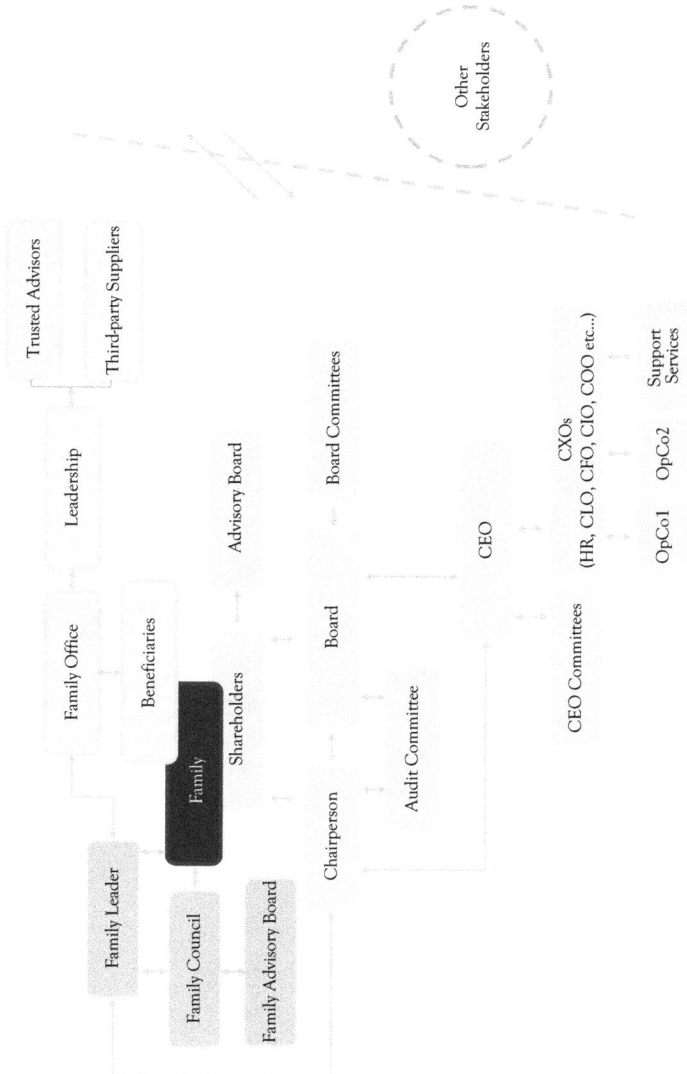

Figure 1.55

You will note that the figure includes both internal and external channels of communication.

Successful communication enables the smooth rotation of the world that gravitates around the family and the business. Each element has a specific role to play. The leader would act as a Chief Communications Officer, ensuring that all these elements act in coordination with one another and that all individuals within a family business ecosystem communicate regularly and respectfully.

Overview of Communication Channels

Communication Channels Within the Business System

Figure 1.56 illustrates broadly the relationships and interaction among the relevant individuals/groups within the business system. Figure 1.57 outlines the communication channels between the family owners and the various systems within the family business.

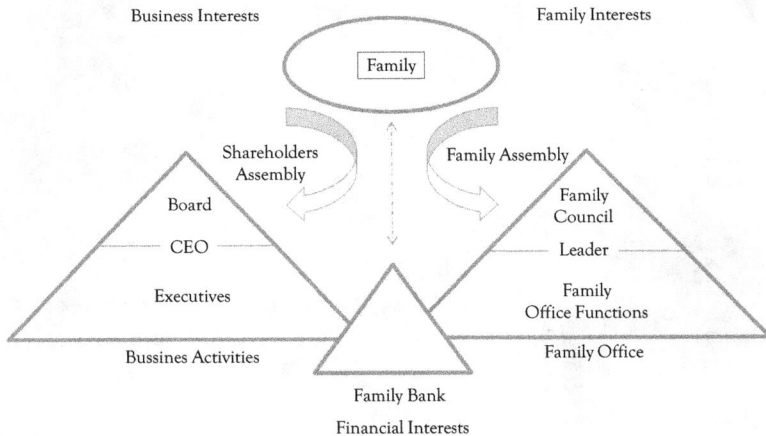

Figure 1.56

Communication Channels in the Family Business Environment

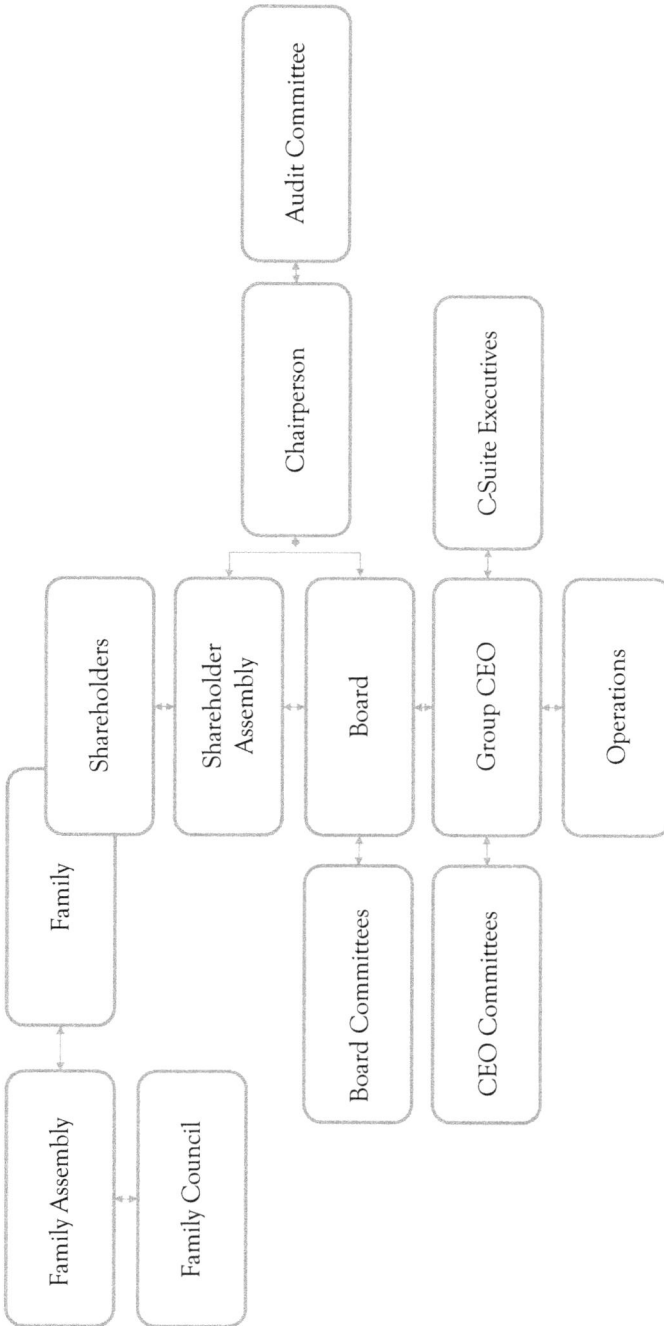

Figure 1.57

Communication Channels Within the Family System

Figure 1.58 details the communication channels between the family members and the various systems within the family.

Communication Channels between Family Members and Various Systems

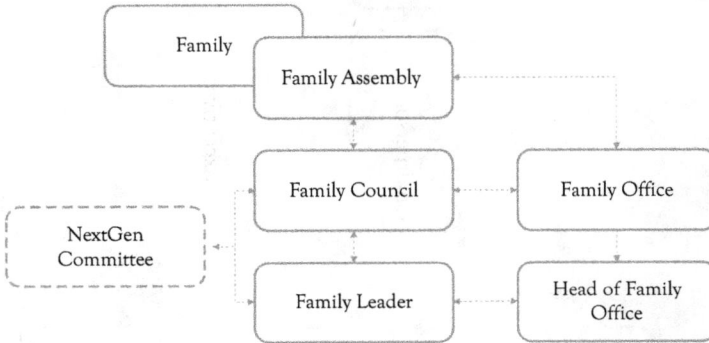

Figure 1.58

Communication Channels between the Business and the Family

Maintaining the link between the business and the family members is important for family members to be made aware of the activities of the business while also contributing, where appropriate, to the identity and culture of the business (see Figure 1.59).

Family Leadership

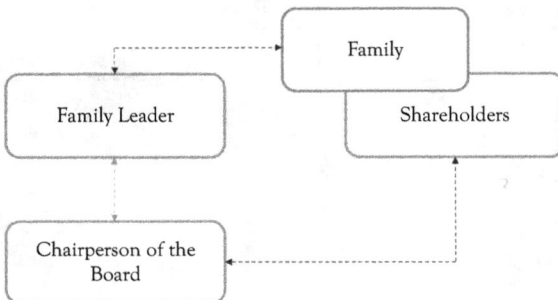

Figure 1.59

As noted in Figure 1.59, it is intended that the family leader carries out this role.

It is recommended that every family business appoints/employs a Chief Communication Officer. This role may fall on the shoulders of any one of the following individuals: the family leader, the Chairperson, the CEO, the head of the family office, or any other trusted advisor the majority of the family is comfortable to have around and is happy to let into their lives.

PART 2

Fundamentals of a Family Charter

As mentioned earlier, a family charter is the culmination of a long journey on which the family has embarked. This is the point where it all comes together in a comprehensive manner. This is the point where family values, family loyalties, family aspirations, and family commitment transcend all uncertainties and compete to become the driving force in maintaining and enhancing the family business.

At this point in time, the family has to come to terms with the following:

- What is it the entire family is encouraged to get involved in and be part of?
- Does the family, individually and collectively, wish to remain united and together build a common project? Can the family's individual members combine their strengths and become the sum total of the entire project?
- If yes, what is this common project? What are the rules that will apply? What will regulate the rights and obligations of each family member in the interest of the family as a whole and in the interest of the family business?

When a family reaches this stage, it is assumed that they have gone through the journey as defined herein, they have attended conferences dealing with the various aspects of a family business ecosystem, and have all done some in-depth reading on the subject matter.

A family can claim success only if they complete these exercises conscientiously, diligently, and seriously and achieves unanimity of the process to find the correct path forward. One dissenting voice beyond this juncture can undermine the whole project.

A family charter is the instrument in which the family will document its findings and will lay out the rules of engagement among them.

A family charter is bespoke. It is tailor-made to fit the needs and the requirements of a given family. It summarizes the compromises and conclusions the family members have reached in order to stay united and build their future together.

The family unit is the sum of all the individuals it comprises, and because every family member is unique, every family unit is unique.

As mentioned earlier, advisors are mere facilitators. A family charter is built by the family, for the family. The advisor's role is limited to helping the family embark on the journey, and go from point A to point B.

At the end of the day, the family needs to "own" its family charter

Contents of Part 2

Part 2 is divided into three chapters, as follows:

Chapter I: Concepts Underpinning a Family Charter
This chapter paves the way for the next two chapters and addresses the various queries we tend to receive from families. The answers provided herein are my own. You will find that some do not match with what is being published elsewhere. Still, I stand by them. They are based on the prerequisite of all sound advice—personal experience.

Chapter II: Typical Table of Contents
This chapter simply lists the topics that are usually addressed under a family charter. This table of contents may be used as a checklist for future reference. It may be supplemented by new topics to reflect the needs of the family.

Chapter III: Select Provisions of a Family Charter—Annotated
It was my initial intention to share with the reader a full-blown family charter. If I had done so, this book would have been a thousand pages long. Instead, I selected five of the most popular topics families tend to discuss and that are often the source of misunderstanding. I added certain annotated sample provisions for illustration purposes.

CHAPTER I

Concepts Underpinning a Family Charter

1. What Is a Family Charter?

A family charter is a tool used to create alignment and a shared vision among the family members who decide to engage in a common project. It documents the *modus vivendi* among the family members, and the *modus operandi* of their business and non-business assets. In other words, it articulates the fundamental rules that govern the relationship among family members, their relationship with their business, and their relationship with their financial wealth.

For all intents and purposes, it is akin to an insurance policy for the family business, safeguarding the capital of a family in all its forms: financial, human, social, and intellectual.

The family charter is a by-product of the journey as outlined in this book. It serves as a tool to document the agreed-upon policies in line with the family's defined group vision and mission, and is a guidebook for the future. While not every conceivable situation can be adequately planned for, a well-devised family charter can aspire to:

- create a sense of direction and purpose;
- put in place systems and policies to preempt events and circumstances that could potentially paralyze the operations of a business or threaten family unity and harmony;
- instill a sense of fairness;
- define the basic principles the family agrees to adhere to and conform with;
- describe the manner in which the family and its business are organized, and are connected;
- define the role of each family member, and their rights and obligations;
- set clear parameters for the exercise of power, define checks and balances, and limit transgressions; and, most importantly
- pave the way for the pursuit of happiness.

A family charter is meant to evolve over time and to adapt to the life cycle and to the growing needs of the family and its business. Its ultimate objective is to ensure the stability, security, and sustainability of both the family and its wealth in the hands of current and future generations.

2. What Is the Difference Between a Family Charter and a Shareholders' Agreement?

A family charter is more inclusive than a mere shareholders' agreement.

A shareholders' agreement is limited in scope. It covers only one aspect of the equation to the exclusion of the others. It is entered into by the individuals holding a financial interest in a given project and provides for the rules of engagement among them. It covers items of interest to the investors, to the exclusion of any other matters, including those that are family-related and others that are family finances-related.

A family charter is more encompassing. It is entered into by all family members. It is a blown-up version of a shareholders' agreement and provides for the rules of engagement among the family members. This applies over three levels: the family, the family business, and the family finances.

3. Is a Family Charter an Adhesion Contract?

Is a family charter deemed to be an adhesion contract? Well, yes and no.

As we discussed in the first pages of this book, a family charter is prepared by the family, for the family, and for its well-being through this and future generations.

When a family first embarks on the drafting of its first family charter, the process should be collaborative and should detail and reflect the desires and wants of the key family members at a given time. The family charter should reflect the spirit and essence of the collective family, and all parties that participated in the drafting and compilation of the charter should be "willing" signatories to the charter given that it is a representation of the collective wants of the family. In this instance the charter cannot be deemed to be an adhesion contract, as the process of drafting it is a participatory one.

However, as the years go by, new family members come into the fold, be it new spouses or NextGen family members who come of age, and these individuals are asked to come on board with the family business and become signatories to the charter.

This is where the participatory process diminishes, and rather the take-it-or-leave-it approach is presented when new signatories are asked to come on board with the pre-defined charter.

Indeed, not all new spouses take it gently when asked to enter into a prenuptial agreement or a family charter. Many would want to consult with their lawyers, and many would come back with a number of questions they would like to see addressed.

The same applies when NextGen members are asked to adhere to a family charter. In many cases they rebel, and try to find ways to assert themselves.

My recommendation has always been to first share the existing family charter and explain the concepts and values underlying each of its provisions, and then ask a new spouse or a NextGen to embrace it. The benefits of a well-constructed family charter will soon become self-evident to all parties.

Sharing the family charter is (1) a sign of respect and (2) gives the new entrant an opportunity to ask questions and contribute new ideas. As said many times throughout this book, dialogue and communication are the glue that reinforces the bond among family members and ensures the sustainability of the rules of engagement they wish to be applied. New ideas will only reinforce that glue and, consequently, reinforce the family commitment.

No one should be expected to adhere to something they do not understand or relate to.

This is where the role of a family leader, or a trusted advisor, becomes crucial, and this is where family values and family culture are put to the test.

New adherents to a family charter are owed the same courtesy as those family members who went through the succession planning journey, and who understood the reason behind each provision, if not of each word in the family charter.

I understand the frustration such requests may generate. But this is fundamentally the reason for having a family charter and for nurturing family culture and family unity. If spouses (wife or husband) do not subscribe to their in-laws' values and sense of ownership, how are they expected to instill the family values into their children?

Wisdom dictates that all family members express their opinions freely and respectfully and that they be taken seriously.

Family charters should adapt to a family's new realities, no matter how often they need to be revisited.

Revisiting the Family Charter

Revisiting the family charter at the whim of every family member or signatory requested to become party to it would diminish its meaning and worth as a "contract."

That being said, a family charter is not carved in stone, and should be flexible enough to evolve with, and adapt to, the family environment while reflecting the new realities of the family.

Therefore, it is advisable, when drafting the charter, to accommodate for certain periods that will allow for the "revisiting" of the charter. This could be once every three, five, or ten years, depending on the family's desire.

That way, all family members are also aware that there will be a certain time period where their voices will be heard and considered, and gives them confidence in the governance process and worth of the charter. Drastic changes do not need to be made to the charter during these periods of revisiting, and policies don't have to change, but it provides an opportunity to provide commentary on the family and business circumstances and provide context for current and future generations.

4. How Long Should a Family Charter Be?

The length of a family charter is irrelevant. It may take several forms and will depend greatly on the *maturity* of a given family and the objectives it wishes to achieve.

As such, a family charter may be limited to a three-word family crest, it may be one paragraph long, or it may also be limited to the expression of general principles summarizing the values of a family in business. Finally, it may be lengthy and detailed, and several pages long. It may be seen not as a rule book, but as a guide book, with each section carefully indexed and easily found when clarification is required to place matters in context and help to settle any dispute.

When discussing family charters, one needs to keep in mind that a family business ecosystem is in continuous motion.

Timing is paramount. The family knows best when it needs to start a dialogue around family charters.

- Where are we in the life cycle of the family and the business?
- What prompted the discussion about devising a charter, today, as opposed to yesterday?
- Who initiated the process?
- Why?
- Are the family members ready (emotionally, intellectually, and physically) to engage in the process?
- Do they know what it entails?
… and so on.

These are among the questions that go to the heart of the matter. They will determine the content and thus the length of the charter, the speed at which it is devised, the unity and solidarity of the family, and its commitment to implementing its provisions.

Our experience has shown that the larger the number of family members, and the older the business, the more detailed a family charter must be.

In our experience, this is due to several factors, the most common being the following:

- Most founders will have difficulty letting go. They will wish to rule "from beyond the grave." They will try to introduce as many of their personal philosophies as possible to underline their achievements and to influence the course of events once they pass on the baton. They strive for perpetual prominence and a sustained starring role. This is their vision of heaven.

- In cases of primogeniture, where the eldest sibling (in most cases a son), who succeeded the founder as manager of the business, wishes to reestablish peace among his/her other siblings who may be grumbling in the background, their claims for a greater say in the decision-making process, or a fairer share of the pie can be amicably resolved by reference to a well-constructed family charter.

- The sudden death of a hitherto omnipresent patriarch/matriarch who "did not find the time" to plan their succession prior to their passing. In most such cases, the surviving family finds itself at the mercy of a well-entrenched *nomenclatura* whose primary objective is often to protect past vestiges and its own self-interests. Piercing the veil will require a clear vision, solidarity, and a strong commitment by family members to take ownership of their inheritance.

- Or, on the contrary, an avant-garde patriarch/matriarch who wishes to plan their succession and wishes to accompany their children throughout this journey, and who invites them in during his lifetime.

- A family with a history of conflict that wishes to protect its own, and instill a sense of unity and stability, in the interest of the business and its stakeholders. Usually, in such a case, families are wary of the past and seek to prevent history from repeating itself. They tend to want to detail every action for the avoidance of doubt.

As mentioned earlier, many of the mandates I have worked on have had an element of conflict in them. Two reasons tend to come up:

1. A lack of communication, leading to misunderstanding the issues and the underlying concepts, and in many cases to a lack of recognition of the needs and wants of each player; and

2. What I call the unresolved relationship with money.

Unfortunately, in many cases, money trumps communication. And all too often, the love of money trumps the love of family values.

Money corrupts and if the division of wealth is not in accordance with an established and agreed format within a family business, it may be the most corrosive element in the family mix.

We have come across situations where seniors would purposely keep their NextGen in the dark and would not share with them the extent of their financial wealth to, in their view, protect the NextGen.

We found that, in general, this lack of financial education and openness is prejudicial and totally counterproductive.

There is nothing wrong with having money or telling the NextGen they come from a family with wealth. A good family charter will ensure that this wealth is used to the benefit of the family and the community it serves.

I am not saying that one should tell their child that they are the son/daughter of a millionaire at the age of two. What I am saying is that children are not stupid and should not be treated as such. They see and observe and form their own opinion. When they are born in a three-story house, and when dad rides in a Rolls Royce, while their school friend lives in a two-bedroom apartment and their dad drives (himself) in a Toyota Corolla, the child starts asking himself questions.

The internet is a child's best friend.

Sharing information, and managing such information, is crucial.

With wealth comes obligations and constraints. The NextGen should be made aware of this from an early age. They should be taught to respect money, and to spend money wisely. With the confidence that wealth brings, compassion should be its constant companion.

Entrusting the management of one's financial wealth to a third-party trustee, as opposed to teaching one's child the value of money and the manner in which they should manage it, is in my view counterproductive and to a certain extent "dangerous." It often has an adverse effect, contrary to the one that is being pursued. It will destroy forever the bond between a child and their parents.

It all starts with good intentions but ends up in tragedy.

The correct relationship with money should be taught at an early age.

After all, no matter how much money you have, you will not be able to take any of it with you to the grave.

Yes, you are free to donate it all, or in part to charity, but should you choose to leave some to your children, you would like your children to respect your hard labor and to take over from you what you have built in a responsible manner. The best way to serve your community is to ensure continual wealth creation within it even after your passing. The old adage that "you give a man a fish, he eats for a day. Teach a man to fish and he eats forever" applies in this scenario.

Once they become the recipients of "your money," it becomes theirs.

Unless they have special needs, and require protection, your role as a parent is to educate your children and provide them with the tools they need to survive in an increasingly unstable and competitive world.

Should you fail in your endeavor, do not blame them for squandering "your" money. In any event the likelihood of you witnessing this is very small.

You just need to have confidence that you have done your best to instill your vision and philosophy in them, and hope that they will mature as you did, excel as you did, and, with your genes pulsing through their souls, their achievements may even surpass yours.

I am not trying to lecture or patronize. I picked up these thoughts from the NextGen and from seniors I have worked with. They are serious about the need to embrace the NextGen as early as possible and train them to deal with money.

As we do not control the day we shall pass, it is recommended to start the financial education of the NextGen "yesterday." But the day before yesterday would be even better!

Parenthood comes with challenges and responsibilities.

5. Is a Family Charter Legally Binding? Is It Enforceable Before Local Courts?

These are the two most common questions families in business typically ask.

Contrary to what you may find in the literature, the answer is a resounding *yes*.

For those families who wish their family charter to be a binding instrument, they can find comfort in contract law.

Many will tell you that a family charter is merely a declaration of good intentions and as such, it is not binding. In my view this is *false*.

Some cynics say that most family business authors are not lawyers. They claim that the ones based in jurisdictions where the legal profession is regulated are terrified of being accused of practicing law without being members of any local bar association.

You may be surprised, however, to see the number of lawyers who say the same thing.

A family charter is charter of trust. Above all, it is a contract, and a contract binds the individuals who entered into it.

For me, any instrument, if validly formed (in compliance with the provisions of applicable laws) and if signed by two parties, is a contract, in conformity with the Roman adage imported into modern contract law since time immemorial (*Pacta Sunt servanda*—the contract is the law of the parties). It is binding among those two parties and it is enforceable before a court of law. While a family charter is not a shareholders agreement, this does not detract from its legal validity when it comes to the rule of law. A family charter, provided it follows the basic principles of contract law and does not contradict the rules of public order, is legally binding. To be valid, and thus binding, the formation of a contract generally requires an offer, an acceptance, a consideration, and mutual intent.

"Going through the motions," as I like to say, just to humor this one or that one, and knowing in the back of your mind that what is being discussed and papered is only for the show is a waste of time, money, and effort. For me, *a person's signature is a person's bond*. Any person who reneges on their signature is not worthy of being my partner.

The same should apply to families who are looking for a mechanism to ensure unity and stability over the years. Keep in mind that entering into a contract is optional. If forced to enter into one, then the contract is null and void.

However, entering into a contract willingly, after weighing the pluses and minuses, and after having been given all the time and the opportunity to ask questions and to participate in debates, leaves a person who signs the contract with no excuse. Under contract law, the option remains to dispute this or that clause after signature. This is utterly legitimate and this is the reason why courts exist. Some families are more litigious than others. For some people, litigation is a way of life. Regardless, this will not take away the fact that a document entered into by two parties is a contract, and that it is binding before a court of law.

A family charter can, and often does, include provisions that are included in more commonly recognized forms of legal agreements such as a shareholders' agreement, and to this end the provisions of a family charter can be legally binding and enforceable.

A family charter also typically includes provisions with regards to soft issues. They serve as morally guiding principles. Due to the nature of such provisions, they may be difficult to enforce or be binding, though they can serve as a useful tool in reflecting the spirit of the document and the intent of the parties.

This is important, as by their very nature, family businesses have the intrinsic element of "familyness" (another term borrowed from the writings of James E. Hughes, Esq.), which does differentiate them from other forms of business. It is my belief that families in business need to learn to embrace the family nature of their relationship even if only from a family (not business) angle.

The law sets minimum standards of ethical behavior, and while it embodies ethical principles, it does not prohibit acts that may be perceived by others as unethical. In a family business where all owners are family members, this may lead to family members feeling that they are being treated unfairly or unethically.

This is a pertinent area in family business because beyond the law, there exists a human relationship and a family bond among and between family members, and between the family and society, and thus the relationship between law and ethics is an important one.

Family values and philosophy will inevitably influence the operation of a family business and will likely lead to a different mix between what is "legal" and what is right for the family and for the family business. As such, a family charter serves as a beneficial tool to address such an overlap.

To this end, the family charter connects the dots between law and family ethics and values, often building on the minimum legal requirements stipulated by the law.

The prerequisites of ensuring the legal validity of a family charter are as follows:

- The provisions of a family charter do not contradict the provisions of the law of the country where the agreement will be executed, nor should it violate the public order of the relevant jurisdictions where it would be implemented.
- The formation of the family charter follows the basic principles of contract law, and encompasses an offer, an acceptance, a consideration, and a mutual intent to be bound. As a result, a family charter that is voluntarily signed by members of a business-owning family having come together to make a set of promises to each other and reach mutual assent is therefore a legally binding and enforceable bilateral contract.
- The mutual assent and voluntary signature of the family charter by all members of the family. *A man's word* (even more so, his signature on a piece of paper) *is his bond*. As such, a participatory process is key when drafting a charter. A charter cannot be prepared by one or two members of the family and imposed on the majority. In such instances, it would be void of the assent that should be voluntarily given by all parties to the contract.

Walid's Insights

At this point, the only advice I can give is the following:

Should you wish to join your family in owning and managing a business, I encourage you and your family to sit around a table and agree common "rules of engagement." Participate actively in the discussions taking place, with an open mind and in good faith (no hidden agendas). Be patient and respectful toward others' opinions. Take time to devise rules that are deemed equitable and with which everyone around the table is comfortable, and would be happy to adhere to. When in doubt, seek help and advice from trusted and competent third-party advisors. Focus on content, as opposed to decorum, use reason and do away with emotions, and most importantly, be truthful to yourself and to the others.

If, at the end of this exercise, you find that you are not satisfied with the answers given, or if your heart is not at peace, then withdraw from the conversation. In this case, and if the subject of debate is an inheritance, then agree on a fair valuation of your share, and go your own way. You will be happier and you will be doing everyone around you a favor.

In matters of inheritance, you always have the choice to accept your share of the inheritance or reject it.

In the event the inheritance is joint with others (e.g., siblings or cousins), you have to choose, either to remain co-owner with your siblings and/or cousins, or ask to subdivide the inheritance (or receive the equivalent in monetary or other value) and go your own way.

If you choose to part ways, then always keep in mind that, no matter what, an amicable compromise is better than a fight in court.

Partnership is optional.

You don't choose your family, but you can always choose your partners, even if those partners happen to be members of your family.

When discussing money with your family, think of your children and the legacy you will be leaving behind.

Act wisely.

If you choose to partner with your siblings and/or cousins, then it would be in your interest to enter into an agreement that would define the rules of engagement among you.

If you decide that the agreement will deal only with the manner in which you wish to manage your common assets, then I would suggest that you limit yourselves to entering into a shareholder's agreement.

If, however, you decide that the agreement among you should go beyond the monetary aspects of your relationship and should deal with your family legacy and the sustainability of your business in the hands of future generations, then I would recommend that you go a step further and devise a family charter.

In either case, it is my opinion that the agreement you will enter into be binding and enforceable before a court of law, as long as it does not conflict with what is referred to as public order.

6. What is a Family Charter Supposed to Achieve?

Running a business and being (or heading) a family are two separate matters, and as such, when the two become intertwined there is a need to create boundaries and rules.

I look at a family charter as a tool to achieve a 3S insurance coverage that would offer a family-controlled business long-term **stability, security, and sustainability**.

Below, I have listed a summary of the main components of the 3S insurance policy. While the coverage required will differ from family to family, typical areas that it should cover are as follows:

- Setting out the core values of the family to which all members of the family should adhere, thus ensuring that the family's identity and cultural capital are upheld
- Setting out the family investment policy in relation to the activities of their operating businesses, investments, and family office, if one has been established by the family
- Defining a succession plan to secure a smooth transition from one generation to the next
- Providing a mechanism for decision-making among the family
- Defining a dividend policy, so that the needs of both the family and business are met and that each family member knows what they can expect to receive
- Providing a way in which the NextGen family members are given responsibility for matters within the governance framework, and providing mechanisms for their employment and integration in company operations
- Providing an agreed-on mechanism for conflict management between family members
- Providing a means for articulating a family's philanthropic vision and putting this into effect

In essence, the family governance framework addresses all the potential "what-ifs" associated with a family business. It addresses the concerns of the different stakeholders within the family structure and it defines the roles and guidelines under which they should operate.

Such a framework must be defined in writing.

To this end, a family charter is more than a hypothetical ideal or a physical or legal structure put in place to safeguard a family's wealth. It encompasses the rules of conduct for a given family, a set of systems and policies by which all involved family members can interact and work together to promote the family's vision and philosophy, while maximizing returns and preserving the family's asset base.

It is important to realize that such a family governance framework cannot be imposed on a family; rather, it must be developed and evolved by the members themselves. In the same way that insurance premiums are based on an actuarial assessment of the risk of the insured individual/ item, there are many factors within each family business that will affect the design and coverage of the 3S insurance policy.

7. What Makes a Family Charter Successful?

A family charter is successful (i.e., is sustainable and can withstand the test of time) when the underlying succession planning exercises are successful.

The success of a succession planning exercise is subject to the following three conditions:

1. Alignment of, and buy-in of *all* family members
2. Embracement of the final output by family members and their trusted advisors
3. Proper implementation of the rules and regulations agreed

For this to be achieved, the parties to a succession planning exercise must have "gone through the motions"; in other words, gone through the 7-Step Methodology™, as outlined earlier, in a systematic, conscientious, and diligent manner.

This is the moment of Truth (with a capital "T").

You cannot build an edifice you expect to last, based on lies and misunderstandings.

As in politics, no legislation is passed, and more so, no amendment to a charter is made, without first going through a debate. In democratic countries, no criticism is spared, and no opinion is hidden. It all comes to the surface. A transparent debate takes place, all is said and heard, and a final vote takes place. Once the majority approves a final text, this text is passed and is respected by others.

The debate is closed. Life goes on. Those who voted in favor of the legislation are usually happy with the outcome and those who voted against accept the outcome, but may from time to time try to put their opinion across.

The legislation will stand as long as the opposition does not have enough votes to overturn it, and open the subject for debate.

This is usually how a democracy operates and how civilized debates are conducted.

What makes a charter successful is (1) the effort the family invests in developing it and (2) its implementation in a fair and structured manner.

The 7-Step Methodology™ respects and recognizes this development.

How important is it to execute (sign) the family charter? Executing the family charter achieves several objectives:

- Proves that all the parties are aligned
- Proves that they respect the efforts and opinions of others
- Proves that they respect themselves

How catastrophic is it when certain members refuse to execute the charter?

It is always regrettable when this happens; however, I am an optimist. For me, participating in the journey is more important than executing the final text. There are cases where family members who go through the motions are still not comfortable signing the final charter. It does not necessarily mean they want to opt out. It simply means that they are not yet comfortable with the outcome of the exercise, and that they have not yet reached a conclusion as to the position they wish to take. Further discussions are required to reach full alignment.

This would not prevent others from signing the family charter. It would encourage the recalcitrant members to join in at their own pace.

CHAPTER II

Typical Table of Contents

Family charters cover a myriad of subjects. Most include, at a minimum, language covering the topics outlined in Figure 2.1.

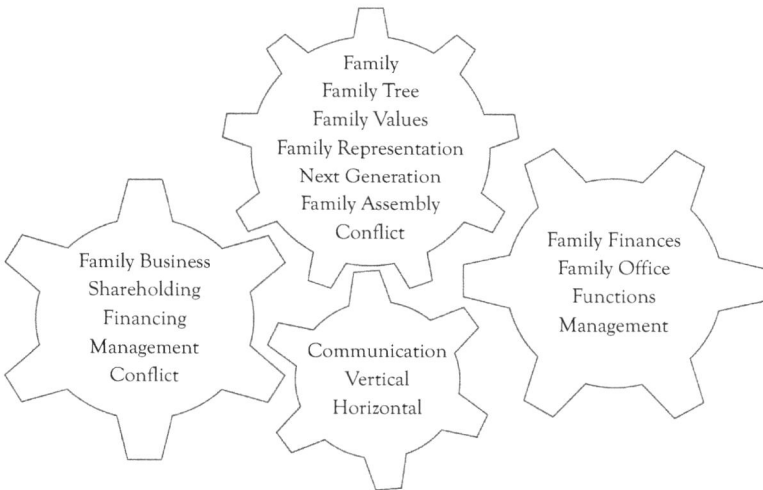

Figure 2.1

A sample table of contents is found below:

General

Alignment

Binding Nature of the Family Charter

Term of this Family Charter

Commitment to Revise Family Charter Periodically

Governance Structure

CHAPTER 1—Family

The Family Tree

Inheritance Matters

The Family History

The Family Values

Significance of the Family Name

The Wider Family

Decision-Making at the Family Level

The Family Assembly

Family Council

Decision-Making Process

The Family Leadership

Family Committees (Investment, Social, Education, and
    Entrepreneurship)

Family NextGen Committees

Family Code of Conduct/Ethics

CHAPTER 2—Family Business

Shareholders

Shareholding Structure

Legal Structure

Bloodline Rules

Shareholders' Rights and Obligations

Entry of New Shareholders

Exit Mechanism

Financing

Capitalization

Financing

Ratios

This is merely a sample.

We invite you to devise your own family charter and to address the topics you believe are important for the family, the family business, the family ethos or "brand," and the family finances.

CHAPTER III

Select Provisions of a Family Charter—Annotated

Chapter III will discuss the following five topics underlying a family charter, namely:

Section 1—Owners vs. Shareholders

Section 2—Delegation of Authority

Section 3—The CEO

Section 4—Family Member Employment

Section 5—Family Offices

I selected these topics because they go to the heart of a succession-planning discussion. They are among those that cause the most confusion and heated debates among family members.

Each section will comprise two sub-sections.

In the first sub-section, I will share my thoughts and findings with the reader, and in the second sub-section, I will share sample provisions.

Some of these provisions have been lifted from actual family charters I worked on.

The language proposed in the next few pages is meant to be illustrative. None of it is sacrosanct. Readers are free to copy the sample provisions provided below, or develop their own, as they see fit.

A family charter must be tailor-made and adapted to address the needs of a given family, not the other way around. One should never seek to fit a family into a charter.

Readers' comments are welcome, and indeed encouraged.

Note: Readers' guide

The sample provisions are found under the heading "Illustration."

Some proposed language is preceded by annotations in italic.

Section 1: Owners vs. Shareholders

Under the section titled "Faux-Amis: Calling Things by Their Name," we showed what we believe to be the difference between a shareholder and an owner.

All the individuals appearing in a family tree (genogram) may be referred to as "owners." Among those individuals, we would need to distinguish between those who are shareholders—that is, those who own a financial interest in the business—and those who are stakeholders—that is, those who have an interest in seeing the business flourish and succeed, but who do not own a financial interest in that business. Parents, spouses, and children usually fall under this category.

Why is this distinction important?

It is important as it helps underscore the sense of entitlement that some members of a family may feel.

"I am an owner … I have the right to sit on the board … I have the right to question the accounts … I have the right to know how much my cousin is earning … I have the right to question the CEO … I have the right to visit the offices when I want …" are comments we hear over and over again from members of the family who either have nothing to do, or are disgruntled and want to make trouble. Most are emotional outbursts, and in most cases their authors ignore the true meanings underlying these concepts.

As a shareholder, you have certain rights and obligations set out under the law. But as an owner, your rights and obligations are more elastic.

Also, if you are not the sole shareholder of a company, it means that you are a co-shareholder, and as a co-shareholder, by definition, you have other partners who each own a percentage of the shares in the business.

Your rights and obligations, as a co-shareholder, are dictated by law, depending on the legal structure you and your partners opt for.

Should you opt for an LLC, as this structure is popular in many civil law countries, then it means that you have decided to retain the decision-making power in your hands (and those of your partners) to the exclusion of any other person, be it the general manager or the board of managers.

Should you opt for a corporation, then it means that you have decided to relinquish the right to make decisions on behalf of the company, and to delegate such rights to a group of individuals you (and your co-shareholders) appoint or elect, to manage the company on your behalf. In this case, whether you appoint yourself to the board is irrelevant. If you do, you will be wearing two hats: one as a shareholder (with rights and obligations), and a second as a board member (with a different set of rights and obligations). Two different bodies and two different sets of rights and obligations. All dictated by law.

Financial institutions often consider LLCs to be an extension of the investors. They believe that LLCs increase their risk of doing business, and they treat them as sole proprietorships. They feel they are dependent on the whims of "individual investors" as opposed to an institutionalized legal entity. To mitigate their risk, financial institutions tend to ask the investors to put up personal guarantees to secure any facilities granted to the LLC.

In a corporation, governance thresholds are higher. They are imposed by applicable legislation. The law imposes a separation between ownership and management, thus granting third-party suppliers a higher guarantee. In exchange, it grants the investors immunity. Their losses are limited to the amount of capital they have invested in the business.

In most countries, the choice of a legal structure is dictated by tax considerations. This section will not discuss taxation. It is limited to discussing general corporate and contract principles. For tax advice, one would need to consult with tax experts.

Should you choose to do so, my advice would be to ask your advisor to adapt the tax structure to meet your family's needs and requirements, not the other way around. Always give precedence to your family, and never compromise their well-being to "save a buck."

"I am the owner … I have the right to …" is an oxymoron under the law.

Again, as a "co-shareholder" in a corporation, you have certain rights and certain obligations that are specifically listed in the law. You do not have the right to manage the company, or even visit the premises of the company, without invitation, nor do you have the right to speak to any member of the staff or receive information, or represent the company in any capacity or act on its behalf and bind it vis-à-vis third parties unless you are appointed a member of the board, or an executive within the company.

Even in such a case, your role is quite limited, as it is defined by law. You do not have free hands.

Family Business Ownership vs. Family Business Shareholding

In this section, it is important to articulate the shareholding structure of the business, both now and in the future. Planning for effective shareholding is key to the sustainability of the family and the business.

Most critically, it is important to decide what ownership means for the family and how ownership is determined; that is, is it a birthright of a bloodline family member or is it something that you have to earn?

Further, it is important to recognize the context of the family's ownership in terms of who are the owners and how they came to be owners. Founding your own business differs significantly from inheriting a business along with various other shareholders (who happen to be family members).

Understanding the Context of Your Ownership and/or Your Position in the Family Business

Beyond knowing your position and role in the business, it is also important for family members to reflect on how they came to their position in the family business, as this also alters their perspective on the business and their relationship with it.

Essentially, the question that begs itself is whether the financial wealth that one enjoys is inherited or is self-made.

Ultimately, titles, ownership, and a position in the family business can be bestowed, inherited, or self-made, and depending on how ownership and positions may have come about, this affects the duties and obligations that individuals have.

Ownership education is an intrinsic part of the succession planning exercise in that it allows the founder to prepare a contingent group of owners who can contribute to the identity of their business based on their wishes, dreams, and vision for the future.

From One Owner to Many

Looking at the family business landscape as it stands today, we note that we are predominantly at a level of a transition of ownership from the first generation to the third generation (skipping the second), and in some cases from the second to the fourth (skipping the third), though tricky at times. Siblings and cousins are taking over from their predecessors, who are in most cases self-made.

Given the exposure to such families in business, there is often a distorted perception of what it means to be an owner in a family business, or to be an employee in the family business.

Where wealth is self-made and self-owned, the founder as an individual, or in some cases, the founders are responsible for their own wealth and the fate of their business. They have built their empire, and can choose to invite individuals to partner with them. They can also choose to carry on alone, and ultimately decide whether to pass it on to their NextGen or dispose of it.

While in corporate terms, business owners owe a responsibility to their stakeholders and the community at large, they do not owe the NextGen anything. They do, however, owe it to themselves to decide what they want for the future of the business and the family and to determine how to get there.

Inheriting a Business/Receiving a Business as a Gift

Additionally, where a business is being gifted or inherited, it is not solely the tangible items that are being transferred. There is the wealth in all its forms (financial capital, social capital, human capital, etc.) that is being transferred, as well as the expectations and the terms and conditions that come with said transfer.

There comes the expectation of how to manage the financial wealth, spend it, and more importantly, of how to live and interact with fellow shareholders, and how to share with them.

These are the responsibilities of ownership that must be defined extensively and thoroughly in order to ensure that all family members are at the same wavelength.

Walid's Insights

In family business ownership, the percentage stake you hold in the business is, to a certain extent, relevant: this has to be placed in the context of emotional ownership. Emotional ownership goes beyond the financial ROI and considers the emotional attachment and sentimental value attached to the business. Family members often feel a sense of pride by being affiliated to the family business and dedicate themselves to the overall well-being of the family business—this is often the case for family members involved in the operation and management of the business. This emotional ownership is also something that can be inherited by virtue of family members witnessing the commitment and dedication of their predecessors.

Emotional ownership is something of significant value to the family business cause, and while it may be difficult to address in tangible terms, it still needs to be managed. Emotional ownership is something that must be instilled in the next-generation business owners and the

*current generation must communicate openly with the next genera-
tion of the business owners about their expectations.*

Determining What Ownership Means for the Family

When devising a family charter, it is essential to reflect on your own views
and thoughts, and engage with the rest of the family to gain their views
and opinions.

Questions to consider and reflect upon:

1. What does ownership mean in terms of your family business?
2. What is the role of an owner?
3. What are the rights and obligations of a shareholder?
4. How will we structure ownership going forward?
5. Do we wish to fragment ownership, or consolidate it within family branches?
6. Is ongoing family ownership in the best interests of the business?

Walid's Insights

*I like to hold interactive workshops around such topics where family
members can actively engage in a conversation around the subject. Usually, workshops range from one to four days, as conversations can become
heated, but it is a process that is invaluable in creating alignment among
the family. I usually assign the family members "homework" in preparation for the workshop, which triggers their thoughts around the topic of
the workshop so that they can serve as the foundation of the discussion.*

The Role of a Shareholder

Upon the passing of title from a senior to several juniors, the juniors, in
addition to being brothers and sisters, and perhaps cousins, become partners instantaneously—that is, co-owners/co-shareholders of an asset, be
it a business or a group of businesses they relate to or do not; they know
or they do not; they love or they do not love.

As a result, the dynamics, and the relationship among these
individuals changes in a fraction of a second.

By virtue of their position as the owners of a financial interest in the business, shareholders have a certain role to play.

While their role in managing the day-to-day affairs of the business is limited, shareholders have certain rights and obligations toward one another and toward the business.

The shareholders of any company have a responsibility to ensure that the company (in other words, their investment) is well run and well managed. This is done by monitoring the performance of the company and raising their objections or giving their approval to the actions of the managers of the company. To this end they have the right to:

- Attend meetings
- Ask questions and vote
- Receive/read information and question the data
- Elect/remove (hold accountable) directors of the board
- Exit/sell shares (as an ultimate sign of disapproval)

The concept of having active shareholders is to ensure that the management and board of companies are accountable for their actions.

The shareholders are the ultimate investors. They have the option to pursue their investment actively or to abdicate their right, and go with the flow. It all depends on what they look for at the end of the day.

Accordingly, in carrying out their duties, shareholders have the option to exercise their rights in various ways, as illustrated in Figure 2.2:

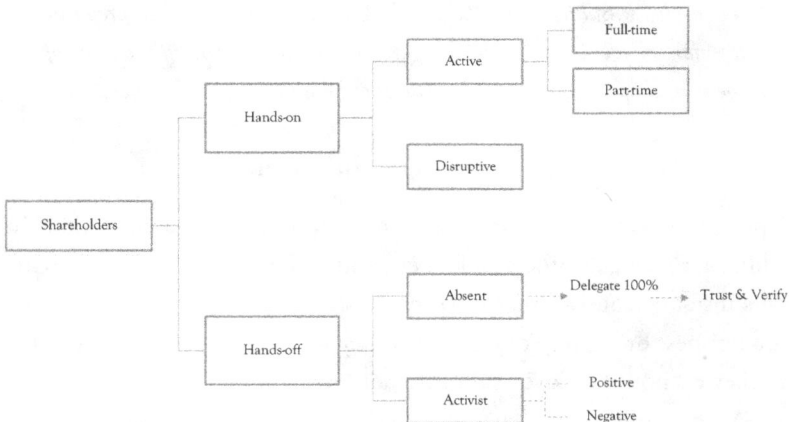

Figure 2.2

Walid's Insights

Often in family businesses where there is a blurring between the role of individuals in their capacity as family members and family shareholders, the role of a shareholder becomes somewhat forgotten or abdicated so as to not disrupt family relations. Typically, in G1- and G2-owned/-managed businesses, family members are employed by the business and/or manage the business affairs for and on behalf of the other family members.

Because of the presence of love, trust, and respect, shareholders do not ask too many questions, do not have too much input, and do not expect much reporting, and as a result are happy to receive the dividends at the end of the year! This always works well until a crisis arises, the most common being that the business faces difficulties and dividends are not as expected, or the amounts are not what the family members are used to.

Then, due to the lack of reporting and forewarning to the shareholders, issues begin to present themselves and questions arise as to why dividends are not as expected. This ultimately leads to a blame game where shareholders who are not involved in the business hold the family members who are involved in the business accountable for essentially not managing the business effectively.

However, what shareholders often forget is that as shareholders they ultimately have a role to play with respect to the business, and where they have not fulfilled their role effectively, they are ultimately accountable.

This being said, shareholders are free to abdicate their right to get involved and to fulfill their obligations. If they do so, there is no one to blame but themselves, if the results fall short of their expectations.

The Owner/Shareholder Assembly

The presence of family owners as shareholders in the family business is often something that is taken for granted. Despite the family relationship, family owners are "investors" who are invested in the business with an expectation of a return on their investment. Should the business not be generating the levels of returns that are expected, family owners, like any other shareholders in a venture, are entitled to withdraw their investment, and seek other avenues they believe will provide a better rate of return.

This being said, some family members are willing to sacrifice their ROI to a certain degree for the sake of remaining part of the family business.

An essential element in the implicit agreement between a company and an investor is that the investor will receive regular, meaningful information on how the company they have chosen to invest in is progressing. Further, they will be invited to vote on decisions that can affect their investment, and others that have been reserved for the shareholders.

Should a shareholder choose to become a passive investor and not exercise their role as defined above, then such shareholder will have no one to blame but themselves in the event the affairs of the business go south.

This being said, the duty to inform a shareholder, even if the latter chooses to be a passive shareholder, is the responsibility of the board and of the chairperson.

Often we hear senior members of the family who hold an executive position complain about the lack of sophistication or financial education of other family members and of their shareholders. In most of these cases, the executives give up on their less-educated family members and neglect to embrace them and educate them.

I am sorry to be the one to break the news: executives have a fiduciary duty to inform, and where appropriate, educate their shareholders, even if such shareholders are family members and are less financially savvy than they are. This comes with the job. You take your shareholders as they come. If this is something you feel you cannot master, then do not take the job.

A family leader, a chairperson, or a head of a family office has an obligation to ensure that all stakeholders receive the information they are entitled to receive, in a timely fashion, and that they are given the opportunity to exercise their rights to the fullest extent.

Failure to do so is a recipe for assured conflict.

At the same time, it is also the responsibility of shareholders to further their education to help them become good corporate and family "citizens." One cannot always blame others for one's faults.

With wealth comes responsibilities, not least of which are education and continuing education.

Family Finances

Retained earnings, shareholder accounts, and dividend policies are intimately related to the subject of ownership vs. shareholding and to family first vs. business first.

They are topics that come up on a regular basis in our discussions with family members and that frequently cause tension among them. This is especially the case if the confusion between what is family (finances) and what is business (finances) lasts for long and is taken for granted with no actual resolution.

Under "Step 6—Know Your Options," the reader was invited to reflect, among other things, on the ultimate objective of having a family business.

"Family first" and "business first" companies differ in the ways that the desires of the family and the needs of the business are prioritized.

It is up to the family to decide whether they wish to put the family first or the business first. Striking the right balance between the two is a real challenge.

For most families in business, the business/family balance is tilted as a result of who the family is, its needs and its values, and where its priorities lie.

For example, one family may prioritize the business over the family, which allows the business to continue to grow, and prosper, in turn providing for the family for generations to come, tilting the positioning of the pendulum further to the right.

Another family may invest more in the family and see the role of the business as an "automatic teller machine" whose objective is to furnish all the needs of the family and allow them to live for the present, tilting the positioning of the pendulum further to the left.

The Balance that Works for You

Of course, where one element is favored, it is often to the detriment of the other element. It is important to find the balance that works well for you and that provides you satisfaction and contentment. The onus is on the ownership system within a family business system to strike and maintain a balance.

Do you feel that needs of the family and the business are both served well, or is there an element that is suffering? If that's the case, there may be something a little out of balance and you may wish to revisit the equilibrium you have created.

For example, if the business is being depleted of cash at a rate where its continuity is threatened, then maybe you may wish to reevaluate your choices. This will depend on the knowledge and awareness of things that are taking place at the business level.

This discussion is important, as we have seen many families sacrifice their long-term well-being in the interest of growing their business indefinitely.

This results in reinvesting all their profits into the business, and accounting for this under "retained earnings."

Reinvesting profits to grow the business must come within the framework of a defined and approved strategy among the shareholders. It is very nice to grow your business and become the largest in this or that, but if this comes at the detriment of the family, you are opening the door wide for long-term catastrophe.

We have witnessed families who have accumulated on their balance sheets substantial "retained earnings" and whose business has failed to generate the profits anticipated in the long term. These families find themselves impoverished when the following three factors happen at the same time: (1) the shareholders wish to cash in, (2) the economy is in deep recession and no exit strategy is available, and (3) the business suffers and is unable to generate enough profit to cover the basic needs of the family.

This is particularly hard on families who have not received their fair share of the profits when the business was booming and who wish to retire from active duty.

It is also hard on heirs, who end up disappointed because they relied on receiving their parents' share of the "investment" upon their passing.

"Retained earnings" are basically IOUs the company issues to its shareholders. They are deferred dividends that are not paid out but reinvested to generate more ROI. When there is no cash at bank to counterbalance retained earnings, families find themselves at a loss.

Educating and later managing shareholder expectations is paramount when accumulating retained earnings.

Defining a sustainable balance between family needs and business needs is paramount.

Continuous dialogue between management and shareholders is crucial to avoid surprises and heartburns when anticipated profits fail to materialize.

Discussions about shareholder loans and advances, capital expenditure, reserves, treasury functions, and dividends are matters for the shareholders to agree with management on regular basis. They are not the privilege of a happy few, especially if management is entrusted to family members. Their duty to inform and their duty to act with utmost prudence are compounded.

My recommendation to family managers: Take the lead and introduce a culture of communication, that is, of information sharing and of open and frank dialogue. Do not hide the truth. Share successes and failures openly and avoid surprising your shareholders at all costs.

For the crux of Smith's insight, I will quote an early reviewer of his book, none other than John Maynard Keynes: "I have kept until last what is perhaps Mr. Smith's most important, and is certainly his most novel, point. Well-managed industrial companies do not, as a rule, distribute to the shareholders the whole of their earned profits. In good years, if not in all years, they retain a part of their profits and put them back into the business. Thus there is an element of compound interest operating in favour of a sound industrial investment. Over a period of years, the real value of the property of a sound industrial is increasing at compound interest, quite apart from the dividends paid out to the shareholders."

—Warren Buffett, letter to shareholders dated
February 22, 2020

Illustration

The topic of ownership vs. shareholding touches on many subjects as illustrated in Figure XX.

1. Family tree/corporate structure
2. Alignment and family vision
3. The binding nature of a family charter
4. Invitation extended to the NextGen
5. Shareholding
6. Bloodline rules
7. Communication
8. Shareholders' assembly
9. Family assembly

Family Tree/Corporate Structure

Note: We are of the opinion that a family charter ought to start with the introduction of the parties.

A family tree or genogram, showing at a minimum three generations of family members, would remind everyone of their roots and would show that there are other people other than "me" who are affected by the provisions of the family charter.

In addition, a corporate structure, showing the business and the various activities, would help illustrate what it is the family has in common and would underscore the efforts and the sacrifices made by the seniors in building such an operation.

Insert a family tree/genogram

Alignment and family vision

Note: Family members who are succeeding a founder (whether by way of inheritance or otherwise) need to decide whether they subscribe to the same project the founder initiated, to their sense of values, and to their vision.

Rare are the founders who create clones of themselves.

In most cases though, the successors need to "take ownership" of the founder's project and make it their own.

They would need to answer the following fundamental questions:

- *What is the project all about?*
- *Do we want to take over the project?*
- *What do we want to do with the project?*

I like to encourage families to start their family charter with an expression of unity and a sense of ownership.

It is important that from the outset they state who they are and what they stand for, beyond being rich, and beyond being the "spouse," or the "sons or daughters of..."

Example 1

Taken from a charter where three brothers (G1 founders of a successful business) decided to pave the way for G2 to succeed them in due course.

- As a family, we believe that we have special family values that have created and contributed to the success of our family business and that have enabled it to be what it has become today.
- We believe it is our role as a family to preserve the family business (and its reputation and standing in the business community) to nurture it and pass it onto the next generations.
- As the first generation, and the founders of the family business, we wish to carry out all the duties and obligations associated with ensuring the security and sustainability of the business in the hands of the next generation.
- We recognize that it is our role to preserve the family business to nurture it and pass it on to the next generations.
- This document reflects our will and desire to devise a practical family and business strategy.

Example 2

Taken from a charter where a family (a sibling consortium) wanted to express gratitude for the gift they had received, as inheritance, from their late father.

- We have inherited from our late father a significant and successful business that has been built by virtue of his entrepreneurial spirit and sheer commitment and dedication.
- We have also inherited values and principles that have contributed to the success of the family business, and that we uphold in all our dealings and day-to-day lives.
- We are extremely grateful for all the endeavors of our late father and the opportunities that he has afforded us, both during his lifetime and beyond.
- Today, our late father's entrepreneurial legacy extends throughout the family business, as well as his priority to enrich the lives of the people who worked with him, and add value to the nation.
- As the (second) generation, and the receivers of this gift, we wish to carry out all the duties and obligations that we perceive to arise from accepting this gift.
- We recognize (with humility) that it is our role to preserve the family business, to nurture it, and pass it on to the next generations.
- We further recognize that we must take responsibility for managing the affairs of the business in a professional manner and select the most qualified individuals—whether from within the family or externally—to help us in achieving our goals.
- This document reflects our will and desire to devise a practical family and business strategy.
- The content of this document outlines our baseline agreements as family members and business partners.

Example 3

Taken from a charter where the family was gifted a large conglomerate by the patriarch during his lifetime.

- As a family, we believe that we have been fortunate and blessed in both a professional and personal capacity and have been presented with unique opportunities in our lifetime.

- The family business is not a birthright we have been gifted with; rather, it is an heirloom that has been entrusted to us for the sake of our children.
- It is our role as a family to preserve the family business, nurture it, and pass it on to the next generations.
- While pursuing our goals, we must ensure to uphold our family's values that are to:
  o Uphold our values in all we do
  o Ensure that the family is above all else in everything we do
  o Maintain strong family bonds and family unity
  o Support each other above personal gain
  o Uphold strong business ethics, transparency, and clarity in everything we do.

- We appreciate that the contribution of [the patriarch] has presented us with unique opportunities in the interest of our community and the environment we live in, therefore we must:
  o Retain and preserve family bonds while ensuring the continuity and operation of the family business as a profitable venture
  o Participate positively and meaningfully as shareholders and family members
  o Develop and enable all family members to achieve their full potential
  o Prepare the third generation to grow together with the same business and family values, such that in time they can "put their stamp on the group"
  o Maintain our family business by pursing collective decision-making
  o Bear the responsibilities and deal with business challenges as a collective majority.

- It is important that we, and future generations, respect one another, uphold the values of the family, and ensure that the family name remains at all times respected by others, including our business associates, employees, clients, and partners.

The Binding Nature of a Family Charter

Note: Confirming the binding nature of the family charter at the beginning of the instrument is essential. It sets the tone from the outset, and it confirms the solemn nature of the instrument being drafted.

- This final document and its counterparts represent a blueprint for succession planning and a commitment by the family to work together to achieve shared goals.
- It is our intention as signatories hereof that this family charter shall have a binding effect among us and our families, and shall replace any and *all* other agreements entered into by the members of the family in the past and by the signatories hereto.
- Furthermore, it shall overrule (among the signatories) any conflicting provisions that may be incorporated in any constituting documents of the group.
- This family charter is in lieu of and incorporates the provisions of any shareholder agreements that might otherwise be entered into by and among the family members and signatories hereto.

Undertaking to Revisit the Charter Periodically

Note: It is important for the family to confirm that their family charter is not carved in stone. It will evolve as the needs of the family, the family business, and family finances evolve. Five years is just for indication, and it could be longer or shorter, depending of the final objective of the family and the complexity of the family dynamics.

This provision is important for several reasons:

- *Formalism and decorum add to the solemnity of the event.*
- *While confirming that the charter is not carved in stone, it is important to send the message to the next generation that nothing should be taken for granted.*
- *It is also important to pass on the message that the set of rules before their eyes has value. It has been devised over time. It has been debated by their seniors, and each provision has its significance. Every clause and every obligation was thought through carefully and was debated.*

If you wish to be part of this venture, please read and understand each provision, its history, and the reason why it has been incorporated.

If you like what you see, you are required to "make a positive act" and adhere wholeheartedly and willingly to the rules. Hence, the importance of the deed of adherence.

- While we wish that the policies herein shall apply indefinitely and that they guide our children, and after that all of the future generations, we undertake to revisit and reconfirm our commitment or amend the policies as may be required every five (5) years from the signature of this family charter.

Invitation to the NextGen to Join

- When any new family member becomes a shareholder, they must undertake to abide by the contents of this family charter. They will be required to sign an agreement of adherence as per the template attached in Appendix XX. Failure to do so would require that they sell their shares in the group in accordance with Section YY.

Shareholding

Note: This provision is important, as it addresses the mindset. We are now moving from just being brothers and sisters to becoming shareholders in a common project.

The family members are putting on two different caps: (1) as siblings and (2) as shareholders.

The dynamics change instantaneously.

The ultimate arbitrator is no longer around. The siblings would need to step up and manage the dynamics themselves.

- As owners of the business, our relationship has evolved from one as siblings to that of being partners and shareholders in a collective venture.

Shareholder Structure

Note: It is customary when a G2 takes over the ownership of a business from G1 to take stock of the status quo.

Previous legal, tax, or financial structures may no longer be applicable. They would need to be adapted to match the needs of each one of the G2 members.

G1 has adopted a certain legal structure that suited their needs at a certain period of time. Upon taking over, G2 would (1) need to acknowledge what has been passed on to them and (2) undertake to amend the structure, where applicable, in the interest of the family members and the family business.

This confirmation is important, as it may have grave financial consequences down the road.

- The current legal and tax structure the business is as follows:
- [Where applicable] It is our intention to amend and upgrade the current structure replace it with the following: …

Bloodline Rules

Note: There are two schools of thought when it comes to allowing in-laws and non-bloodline relatives to become shareholders by way of inheritance.

The liberal school welcomes all members of the family, whether bloodline or otherwise, to become shareholders and contribute to the well-being of the family and the growth of the family business. The liberal view provides that what is good for a family member is good for the family at large. It respects the choices of a family member and agrees to honor those choices after their death.

The conservative view is that in-laws have no place in the business. They are welcome around the dinner table, but not the boardroom table.

The conservative view prefers not to mix family with business. Extreme views question the motives of in-laws. Did they marry the family member for love or for money? It's a dilemma that cannot be resolved rationally.

Under this school of thought, in-laws are permitted in the family business by invitation only. They are treated like non-family employees.

- It is our intention to keep the ownership of our family business within the direct bloodline descendants of our late father. Therefore, while shareholders may gift and sell shares to each other, it is agreed that shareholders cannot gift or sell shares to non-family members.
- On this basis, we acknowledge that it is our wish that our spouses do not own any shares in the business. Having said this, we want to ensure that our spouses are well provided for in the event of the death of a family shareholder.

Communication

Note: Open, frank, and continuous communication is the secret of success of family businesses.

Without open and democratic dissent, conflict will ensue, and in the long run, bad feelings, apprehensions, tensions, and mistrust will settle.

Once the virus of mistrust is implanted, nothing will remove it.

As mentioned above, trust is earned by way of deeds and acts, throughout one's life. It is lost in a fraction of a second.

Trusting and mistrusting are a state of mind.

They are emotional.

Once the trust is lost, it becomes a mission impossible to reinstate it.

The only way to maintain trust is to communicate on a regular basis, in a truthful and professional manner.

Communicating for the sake of communicating, or delegating communication to a non-family member when a family member is a decision-maker, is often interpreted as a sign of disrespect, and may have an adverse material effect on the relationship between those family members who are working in the business, and those who are not.

The forum made available to the shareholders (those who hold a financial interest in the family business) to meet at least once a year, or as many times as they decide in the family charter or the constituting documents of the company.

As discussed above, in the case of a corporation, the decision-making powers rest in the hands of the board of directors. The latter has unlimited powers to bind the company and engage its liability, as it pleases, unless such powers are limited by the shareholders.

The "reserved matters" are those matters that would require a higher percentage at the shareholders' level before they are effective.

The list of reserved matters is not public. Third-party suppliers are not aware of it and are not bound by its provisions.

Should a board of directors overstep its powers, it can be reprimanded by the shareholders. Third-party suppliers are not held responsible should the board overstep its powers, unless they are informed in advance of the limitation of powers of the board.

In a family business, it would be wise for third-party suppliers to obtain confirmation (a representation) from the board of directors and from the executives that indeed they have the power to bind the company.

- As family members, we acknowledge the importance of open communication and we will at all times present all family members with the opportunity to raise their views and opinions in an open, honest, and respectful forum.
- As shareholders, we will ensure that there is an effective system for open and transparent communication so that the wider family feels properly informed about the activities of the various bodies of the business.
- Notwithstanding the above, we recognize the complexities of managing a family business, and, more specifically, the intricacies of maintaining the boundaries between the business and the family.
- In light of this, we are aware of the importance of separating business affairs from family affairs to ensure that each is adequately addressed.
- A governance structure that adequately separates business affairs from family affairs is especially important for us, given our newly found role as shareholders of the business.
- As such, we wish to ensure that we establish all the necessary governance platforms that are integral toward ensuring:

o Open, transparent, and respectful communication
o The separation of ownership from management
o That the needs of the group are adequately addressed and met
o That the needs of the wider family are adequately addressed and met
o That shareholders and the wider family are kept informed of relevant matters on a regular basis

The Shareholder Assembly: Purpose

Note: Shareholder meetings are formal forums open only to those who hold financial interests in the family business. It is a work environment. It is not intended to be a family gathering or a venue to meet "uncle" whom we have not seen for a while.

The number of meetings is optional. Most legislation provides for a minimum of one meeting per year and provides for extraordinary meetings to be held under certain circumstances, in case of emergencies, or in cases as prescribed specifically by law.

- The shareholder assembly is the superior body of governance through which we, as family shareholders, assert our rights with regard to the group affairs.
- [While we have chosen to appoint a board of directors to direct the affairs of the group, we also wish to reserve certain matters "reserved matters" that would require a "special majority vote" of the family shareholders.]

Membership and Meetings

Note: If the shareholders agree to meet once a year, this date usually coincides with the date of completion of the audit reports by the company's auditors. Most legislation provides broad language, and in many countries, the financial year-end of a company is left to the discretion of the company, as may be dictated by its business activity. Usually, shareholder meetings are held at a maximum within three months from the completion of the audit reports.

The audit reports are usually completed within three months from the financial year-end.

At shareholder assemblies, the shareholders have certain specific tasks to achieve.

These tasks are listed in an agenda, given to the shareholders well in advance of the meetings.

Should they have any questions, or should they wish to add an item to the agenda, they should communicate with the company secretary.

No item, other than those provided for in the agenda, can be discussed at the shareholder assembly.

- Only shareholders are allowed to attend the shareholder assembly.

Note: The more nascent the governance rules, the more frequent the shareholder meetings. Always keep in mind that management is working in the interest of the shareholders. The latter need to feel confident that their managers have their interests at heart.

Investors do not like uncertainty, nor do they like surprises.

The dates provided below are for indication purposes only. Businesses may have different financial years and as a result can amend those dates to fit their own needs.

- The shareholder assembly shall meet [twice] a year at a minimum, once at the latest by [December 31], to:
  o Discuss performance and historical results
  o Agree on the business plan for the coming twelve (12) months.

- Once at the approximate mid-point of the year, at the latest by [June 30], to:
  o Approve year-end accounts
  o Review budgets
  o Approve the declared dividend

   o Receive mid-year financials and performance updates
   o Elect/renew the mandate of board members.

- The shareholder assembly shall also meet at any other time where a shareholder resolution is required.
- A minimum of four (4) weeks' notice shall be given to members of the shareholder assembly ahead of a meeting.
- If an extraordinary meeting of the shareholder assembly is required at short notice, then a minimum of one (1) weeks' notice shall be given to members.
- In calling a shareholder assembly, the chairperson shall prepare a written notice ("the invitation") stating the location, date, time, and agenda of the meeting and the matters to be proposed at the meeting. The invitation, together with the related documents, shall be delivered to the shareholders at least seven (7) days prior to the date of the meeting.
- Any shareholder shall have the right to propose adding an item for discussion on the agenda, as long as the notification of this item is made three (3) weeks prior to the date of the meeting.

Note: The chairman of the board is also the one who will chair and conduct the shareholder assembly.

A certain decorum must be respected to avoid chaos and to ensure the proper and orderly advancement of events.

- The chairperson of the board shall chair the meetings at a shareholders' assembly. In the event that the chairperson is not present at a meeting or cannot perform their duties, the shareholders present at the meeting shall elect one (1) shareholder from among them to chair the meeting.
- A meeting of the shareholders is considered quorate if the shareholders owning over fifty percent (50 percent) of the capital stock of the company (or their relevant proxy) are in attendance.

- If a meeting of the shareholder assembly is not quorate, the meeting will be reconvened seven (7) days later, at the same place and at the same time to address the same topics as listed on the agenda. The shareholders in attendance at this meeting shall constitute the quorum, irrespective of the number of shares they hold (or the percentage) in the capital stock of the company.
- Where technology permits, it shall be possible for the shareholders to attend a shareholder assembly by way of a telephone call, voice-over-IP call, or any other similar technology medium as the shareholders may agree, provided that the shareholders can hear and be heard in real time.

In order to preserve the balance and avoid any one shareholder monopolizing the voting power:

- A shareholder who submits a vote by proxy shall be regarded as present at the shareholder assembly. A shareholder can issue a proxy only to another shareholder who is a family member.
- Any one shareholder shall be allowed to hold a proxy on behalf of one (1) other shareholder.
- The proxy appointment must be in writing. The duly completed and executed proxy form shall be delivered to the chairperson before the commencement of the meeting.

Decision-Making

- The shareholder assembly can only vote on items that are listed on the agenda, unless the shareholders attending the meeting agree unanimously to add such an item to the agenda.
- Voting shall occur in accordance with the number of shares each shareholder holds in the capital stock of the company.
- Resolutions may be passed by way of circulation of a written document (including, but not limited to, courier, fax,

or e-mail). In this case, the chairperson shall confirm the signature of each shareholder individually, and the number of shares each such shareholder holds in the capital stock of the company.

Special Majority

Note: We prefer to avoid unanimity, to avoid deadlocks, as well as the possibility of blackmail by disgruntled family members. In the event of a conflict, the chairperson would be required to play an active role in diffusing tensions.

- A special majority vote shall require that shareholders representing eighty percent (80 percent) of the financial interests of the group vote in favor of a reserved item in order to pass a resolution. Reserved matters are those items defined in Appendix 2.

Simple Majority

- All other matters that require the vote of the family shareholders shall require a simple majority vote (50 percent +) of the financial interests of the group to pass a resolution.

Note: We propose you revisit this percentage, in the event one of the shareholders has a controlling bloc of shares.

- Where it is not possible to obtain the necessary votes to pass a resolution, the chairperson shall take the matter under advisement, and shall decide whether (1) to discuss said matter separately with the shareholders following the conclusion of the shareholder assembly or (2) include the matter for discussion on the agenda of the next shareholder assembly.

Purpose of the Family Assembly

Family Assembly

Note: Family assemblies, or family get-togethers, differ from shareholder assemblies in the sense that they group all family members, shareholders and non-shareholders. It is the only forum that spouses and parents can attend.

They can also attend family councils, if they are elected to join such a body.

- The family assembly provides an opportunity for all members of the family including the wider family to gather, spend time together, and bond. It is a forum in which to discuss the family ethos, vision, and values, and share these with the wider family. No monetary or operational details regarding the family business will be discussed at family assemblies.

Family Assemblies

Note: Family assemblies should be formalized and treated seriously; otherwise, chaos would follow and no serious conversations will take place.

They need to be results oriented.

Family members need to vote and understand what it is they are voting on, and why. They need to feel empowered, and with empowerment comes accountability.

The family assembly:

- Operates as a platform where all family members are able to voice their opinions and ideas on matters related to the group and the family;
- Allows all family members to contribute to decisions relating to the family business interests;

- Ensures continuity and stability from an "ownership" perspective, and ensures that a proper framework exists to introduce the NextGen into the family business;
- Passes on the traditions, culture, and values of the family and the business to successive generations;
- Establishes the civic, political, and philanthropic roles of the family;
- Upholds and carries out the family's charitable commitments and duties;
- Encourages and supports new ideas from the family;
- Upholds the values, vision, and philosophy of the late patriarch and the family owners;
- Ensures that the family charter is updated as and when required, and that the incoming generations have an opportunity to add and amend when the need arises;
- Is the guardian of the family ownership system, and shall:
  o Define the rights and responsibilities of ownership
  o Establish the family policy for transferring ownership
  o Monitor the interests of all family members; and
- Is minimal with respect to any business-related matters. It shall be the responsibility of the shareholder assembly to carry out the functions and responsibilities of the shareholders and proceed with the affairs of the business.

Membership and Meetings

Note: This provision may come in handy when you have large families. Establishing rules will reduce the risk of chaos.

Acknowledging family members and their achievements is paramount. Dealing with them with respect is the key to avoiding conflict.

- All family members, including spouses and children, shall be invited to attend the family assembly.

- There shall be at least one (1) annual gathering, between one (1) and three (3) days long (the first such event shall take place on XXX).
- In addition to the annual family gatherings, other social gatherings shall be held.
- Meetings/gatherings shall be funded by the [Family Office]. There shall be a minimum of one (1) family assembly meeting per annum.
- Members of the family assembly shall elect from among them a family leader ("Family Leader") who shall chair meetings of the family assembly and the family council and act as the family leader.
- Any member of the family has the right to add an item for discussion on the agenda as long as the notification of this item is made two (2) weeks prior to the date of the meeting.
- Invitations to sessions of the family assembly meeting shall contain:
  o The date and location of the meeting
  o The proposed agenda
- A minimum of four (4) weeks' notice should be given to members of the family assembly ahead of a meeting.
- The final agenda for meetings of the family assembly shall be circulated two (2) weeks prior to the family assembly, and meeting materials five (5) working days prior to the meeting.
- Minutes shall be prepared for each meeting of the family assembly not later than within eight (8) working days after the day of the family assembly meeting, and shall be signed by all members present at the meeting.
- Meetings of the family assembly shall normally take place at a place and at a date as defined by the family council.
- The preparation of family assemblies/gatherings shall be delegated to [cousin X] [a committee to be formed from among senior and junior members of the family], as may be directed by the family council.

Decision-Making

- It is intended that resolutions shall be reached by consensus at the family assembly.
- If a consensus cannot be reached, we shall conduct a vote by way of a show of hands. A simple majority vote (50 percent +) of those attending the family assembly shall be needed to pass a resolution.
- In situations where a deadlock occurs, the family leader shall have a casting vote.
- Upon the establishment of the family council as described (below), the role of the family assembly shall become an advisory one, whereas the family council shall be a decision-making forum.

Section 2: Delegation of Authority

Having established the need to separate family from business and having identified the necessary platforms and forums, it is important to determine the role and composition of each and to understand the rules of operation.

From a corporate angle it is important to understand the (1) interaction between the shareholders, the board, and the executive management; and (2) the relationship between them all.

Figure 2.3 illustrates the basic interaction and relationship between the appropriate forums.

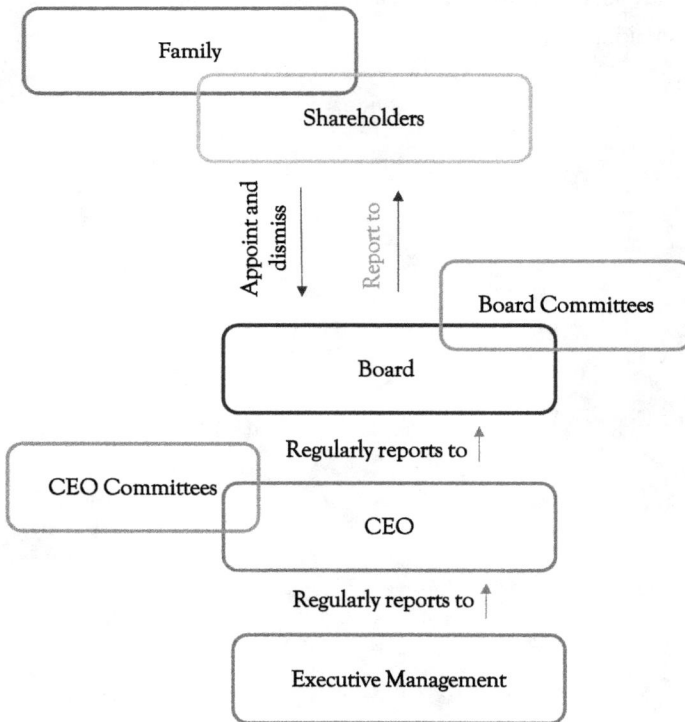

Figure 2.3

The Board of Directors

Over the years, many new rules and guidelines pertaining to board composition and duties have come into being. The bedrock challenge for directors, nevertheless, remains constant: Find and retain a talented CEO possessing integrity, for sure, who will be devoted to the company for his/her business lifetime. Often, that task is hard. When directors get it right, though, they need to do little else. But when they mess it up…

—Warren Buffet, letter to shareholders, February 2020

The board of directors is a first line of defense. It is the tool of checks and balances *par excellence*.

Before building a board of directors it is important to understand what a board does, and whether the shareholders need one.

Not all family businesses need, or are ready, to have an IBM-style board of directors. Some are content with a hybrid-type board, combining the functions of a shareholder assembly and those of a board of directors. Others need a longer time to transit from a private and collegial decision-making forum to a more formal one.

Regardless of circumstances, once the shareholders decide they need a board, they would need to determine what kind of board their business needs, and what kind of board the shareholders can work with.

Most legislation is silent when it comes to determining the composition of the board, the profile of the board members, or the tenure of the directors. As a result, there is no fixed or unique formula for a successful board.

The answers to these questions will depend on the needs of the business over an extended period of time.

Prior to determining whether a family needs a board to take over the management and oversight of their family business or not, it would be interesting to explore what a board actually offers the family and shareholders/owners from a family business perspective.

We are of the opinion that having a board for the sake of having one, and not utilizing it as it should, is a waste of time, money, and energy.

Indeed, many families we know think that they do not need a board, and most believe that such a tool is useless. They are the shareholders, they own all the assets, and they know best.

This may be true at the startup phase of a given business, but unfortunately, over time complacency settles in, and mistakes are made.

So, what can a board offer?

The board may offer, *inter alia,*

1. The family
   - *Independent oversight*: Removes emotions from the decision-making process.
   - *Professional approach*: It does the "homework."
   - *Checks and balances*: It regulates shareholder access and influence over decision-making.

2. The shareholders/owners
   - *Ownership neutrality*: Removes emotions from decision-making.
   - *Institutionalized approach*: Regulates shareholder access to and influence over the decision-making process.
   - *Protection*: from "irrational exuberance."

Once a family decides it needs to appoint a board, it would need to investigate the various factors that must be taken into consideration when building a board of directors. Not every member of the family qualifies to sit on the board, and not only family members qualify to sit on the board (see Figure 2.4).

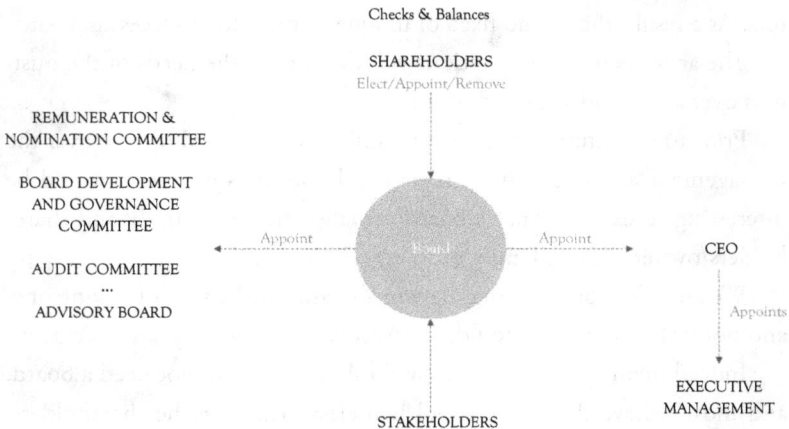

Figure 2.4

Early on, families should widen their scope and identify the most qualified individuals who can assist them in managing their business. They should not fear recruiting non-family members and non-executives to sit on the board. To give them comfort that neither will take the till and go home with it, they should (1) find the best talent out there and (2) introduce effective checks and balances (the famous *trust and verify* theory of Ronald Reagan) mechanisms to reduce risk.

Most of the family businesses we have worked with tend to want to appoint family members to the board.

Sometimes, this defeats the purpose.

The questions below will help guide your thinking with respect to the board of directors and its members:

1. What is the desired level of family involvement in the business?
2. What skills do family members have to contribute (if any)?
3. Where are these skills best used?
4. Who are the right people to direct the family business?
5. What skills will the business benefit from/is the business lacking?
6. Where do we wish to take the business in the next 5–10 years?
7. How are we going to get it there, and what types of challenges are we likely to face? (Think of the black swan.)

Walid's Insights

Board composition is a direct reflection of the owning family's requirements. The composition of the board depends solely on what the family wants from the board and its success ultimately depends on trust and maturity.

Trust is not an article of faith among family members/owners/shareholders/management/employees/directors.

Trust is a product resulting from reliability, predictability, transparency, aligned visions, shared goals, and resultant bonds, and to this end, trust must be cultivated.

In parallel, board composition will evolve as the maturity of the family evolves. The more self-confident the family members are, the more they are willing to appoint non-family non-executives on the board. Ideally, over time, the number of non-family non-executives (independents) will trump that of family members. In some cases, it would be advisable, at least during an interim period, to appoint a chairperson from among family members. This will secure proper communication with the family and would ensure the values of the family are respected by the board.

Tips: Should you find that certain family members insist on controlling the decision-making process, we would strongly recommend enlarging the circle of decision-makers. Add more people around the table. Outsiders.

An outsider's experience and perspective should always be a priority (one way of doing this, for example, would be to expand the number of board members from five to seven).

Illustration

This chapter touches on two important "institutions": the board of directors, on the corporate side; and the family council, its counterpart on the family side.

Board of Directors

Purpose of the Board

Note: Most corporate legislation provides that the management of a company rests with the board of directors.

This will underscore the fact that the buck stops with the board and not individual shareholders.

- In the interest of separating ownership from management and emotion from reason, the shareholders recognize that the management of the business (save reserved matters) shall at all times be the sole responsibility of the board of directors ("the Board") and of the executives as appointed by the board.

Note: The board has several functions.

- The board shall be responsible for the supervision of the affairs and the management of the company. It shall provide strategic direction and oversight of the activities and performance of all business activities.
- *Governance*
  o Sets the strategic vision and mission of the business with a view to ensuring wealth preservation and growth while meeting the present and future needs of the family as set out in the family charter.
  o Appoints/dismisses CEOs.
  o Reviews adequacy of governance arrangements across the business and ensures that these are functioning effectively.
  o Approves an authority matrix for all financial and non-financial matters.
  o Makes recommendations to the shareholders on all reserved matters that are outside the authority of the board.
  o Approves all policies and procedures of the business and ensures that wherever possible these are consistently applied.
  o Approves all recommendations and information that are presented to the shareholder assembly and/or family assembly.
  o Establishes and periodically reviews the mandate and direction of the business and ensures that it has the necessary financial capabilities and human capital to deliver on these goals.
  o Reviews the progress of all major investment projects and change initiatives.
  o Establishes subcommittees (Audit, Investment, Nominations, Project Execution, etc.) as and when required, and receives regular reports on their activities.

- *Financial*
  - o Reviews and approves business plans and budgets of the business.
  - o Approves the annual budget for the business.
  - o Monitors financial performance and key risk exposures of the business.
  - o Receives regular reports from management.
  - o Recommends to the shareholders the appointment of external auditors for the company.
  - o Periodically receives and reviews fair valuations of assets and liabilities.
  - o Recommends annual dividend payments to the shareholders.
  - o Prepares annual financial statements for the company.

Membership and Meetings

Note: The composition of the board depends to a great extent on the timing of when a professional board is being put in place.

In companies where management is a "one-man show," the board of directors becomes futile.

It usually takes a while for a family to buy into and to adapt its habits to embrace new governance concepts.

Moving from a one-man show and agreeing to put in place a board of directors to control and question the CEO is a big step forward.

Usually, a family business grows gradually.

A first board usually comprises family members.

After a certain period of time, non-family members are admitted to the board.

Sometimes, families accept to appoint executives such as CEOs. Or CFOs to their board, as a first step.

There are two schools of thought: one conservative, which is of the view that C-suite executives have no place on the board; and another liberal, whose view is that the shareholders are the ultimate decision-makers. They choose whomever they see fit to help them achieve their objectives.

Conservatives are of the opinion that C-suite executives have a well-defined forum to express themselves and to act. They favor fresh blood and an independent body to engage in proper checks and balances. Should a CEO sit on the board, who shall then hold them accountable, and who will judge their performance? A conflict of interest would ensue and objectives of introducing governance rules would be frustrated.

We are in favor of term limits.

Most laws provide for term limits for board memberships and tenure.

Some jurisdictions provide that the CEO shall be the chairperson of the board. In this case, the CEO becomes a board member, subject to the term limitations as applied to a board member.

Lifetime positions should be abolished and banned in family businesses.

You may own or co-own the financial interests in a given business, but it does not make you the most qualified person to manage this business. Fresh blood should be encouraged and welcome.

Empowerment comes with accountability and responsibility.

- The board will be composed of [...]

Note: In most jurisdictions, it is provided that board members are elected/appointed by the shareholders.

The board members choose from among them a chairperson.

In family businesses, and in most cases, the chairperson is a family member. They are the guardian of the family brand.

- The first board shall comprise the following directors:
[XXX];
[XXX];
[XXX]; and
[...].
- The terms for board members shall be XXX years.
- Board members may submit their candidacy for reelection.
- Any director may serve a maximum of three (3) terms.

Note: Same as with shareholder assemblies, there is a certain decorum to observe.

Board members need to meet more often than shareholders.

They appoint the CEO, give them a certain mandate, and ought to check on the CEO from time to time, and ensure the orderly performance of their duties.

They need to keep their fingers on the pulse of the business, and support the CEO where practicable.

The board shall meet four (4) times per year at a minimum. Any member of the board can request the chairperson to call for ad hoc and additional meetings.

Where technology permits, it shall be possible for a board member to attend a meeting of the board by way of telephone call, internet, voice-over-IP call, or any other similar technology medium as the directors may agree from time to time, provided that the remote director can hear and be heard in real time.

A minimum of fourteen (14) days' notice shall be given to directors ahead of a meeting.

In calling a meeting of the board, the chairperson shall prepare a written notice, "the invitation," stating the location, date, time, and agenda of the meeting. The invitation shall include a management report prepared by the CEO and their executives, under the supervision of the CEO, and the matters to be discussed at the meeting. The invitation, together with the related documents, shall be delivered to the directors at least seven (7) days prior to the date of the meeting.

- Matters not on the agenda, and any business conducted in relation to those matters, may not be raised at a meeting of the board unless all the directors present at the meeting agree. The board shall in all circumstances obtain the approval of the shareholders before taking any decision in relation to any of the reserved matters.

Note: In some cases, board meetings are necessary prior to their scheduled time.

The chairperson of the board shall chair the board meetings.
- The first chairperson of the board shall be [XXX].
- A meeting of the board is considered quorate if two-thirds (2/3) of the directors are present. No business shall be conducted at any meeting of the board unless a quorum is present during the entire meeting.

- If a meeting of the board is not quorate, the meeting will be reconvened seven (7) days later, at the same place and at the same time, to address the same topics as listed in the agenda.

Decision-Making

Note: Unlike the case of shareholder meetings, where the votes are based on the number of shares held by the shareholders, at board meetings, the votes are based on the principle of "one man, one vote."

A family member who owns shares in the business and who is a board member cannot overrule a non-family board member.

That family member will have one vote at the board meeting, irrespective of the number of shares they may own.

- Resolutions shall be passed by a simple majority vote (50+) of the directors present at the meeting.
- Whereas the board will not be responsible for the resolution of family conflict, nor will it be involved in family affairs, it will, when necessary, make recommendations to the family assembly and/or maintain open communication with the family leader.
- Although family activity will not pertain to the key roles and responsibilities of the board, the board shall have regard for the following:
  - o Overseeing the family's involvement in the business
  - o Helping to see that the family's reasonable long-term goals (as the board defines "reasonable") for the business are met
  - o Mediating the family's influence on the business so that neither the financial and employment needs of the family nor family conflicts endanger the long-term viability of the business
  - o Providing helpful mentoring and feedback to family managers, especially where such support is difficult to obtain from managers within the company

Family Council

Purpose of the Family Council

Note: In large families, one may wish to channel the decision-making process in the hands of a few.

One idea would be to set up a family council (board) and grant such body an enforceable decision-making power.

The family assembly would then become a consultative body.

- It is anticipated that once the number of family members attending the family assembly exceeds XXX, we will establish a family council to channel all decisions made on behalf of the family.
- The family council shall carry out the same role and functions as the family assembly.
- The family council shall hold a decision-making role, whereas the role of the family assembly shall be consultative.

Membership and Meetings

- Membership of the family council shall [constitute one (1) representative from each family branch] [comprise (XXX number) elected by the family at the family assembly].

The Family Leader shall chair the Family Council and the Family Assembly.

- The family assembly and the family council shall be used as forums to address family matters.
- We recognize that some family members will share the same values, or the same vision. In this case, the family council shall guide the family on three (3) levels:
  o *Individual*: Supporting those family members who seek help in determining their own personal and professional goals

- o *Family*: Defining the overall goals of the family and the resources needed to achieve those goals and objectives
- o *Business plans* (high-level): Addressing issues dealing with ownership, family control, and involvement in the business, managing expectations, and liaising with business leaders

Decision-Making

- At meetings of the family council, resolutions shall be taken by way of a show of hands. A simple majority vote (50 percent +) is needed to pass a resolution.

Section 3: The CEO

Strategically, a major function of the CEO is to look for bad news and encourage the organization to respond to it. Employees must be encouraged to share bad news as much as good news.

—Bill Gates

A CEO is the Commander-in-Chief. The ultimate *decider*.

When asked what he believes the role of a CEO should be in a corporation, Carlos Ghosn, the once-CEO of the Renault-Nissan-Mitsubishi alliance, said: "A CEO's main responsibility is to (1) run the business, (2) grow its revenue, and (3) do it consistently. Anything else he would be asked to do, would derail him from his main task."

A CEO is the one entrusted with the day-to-day operations of the business, under the watchful eye of the board of directors. If given enough elbow room to act as they please, a CEO becomes accountable for all their acts. Proper checks and balances will ensure no slippage or abuse of power takes place.

In terms of the delegation of power in the business, it is useful to clarify the role of the CEO, particularly in a family business context where it is often the case that a family member assumes this position.

In this event, it is useful to ensure that there is a job description in place for the CEO and that there are key performance indicators (KPIs) in order to measure their performance.

Considering the appointment of, or having, a non-family CEO involves a certain mindset and as with the board, requires trust, respect, and a dose of maturity.

The most obvious reason for appointing a non-family CEO is the existence of a gap in the skillset, knowledge, and experience of family members. A non-family CEO would fill those gaps, in the interest of the family and the business.

The other reason may be the avoidance of a conflict of interest. A conflict of interest may arise should a CEO report to a board comprising executives who report to the CEO on day-to-day matters, and whose remuneration and bonus depend on the goodwill of the CEO.

Some people would even advocate that it is always easier to fire a non-family CEO than a family member CEO should they fail to perform as expected.

The CEO vs. the Chairperson

In family businesses, it is not uncommon for a single individual to hold both the CEO and the chairpersonship positions. This combined role is usually a default result of the CEO as the de facto leader of the business.

A pertinent discussion with respect to the governance of family and nonfamily businesses is whether the role of CEO/chairperson should be combined or separate—with no conclusive correct answer.

From a family business perspective, when the CEO's position is held by a family member, it is important to assess whether a dual CEO/chairperson position is appropriate, particularly when the individual is acting in the interests of numerous family shareholders and is not a founder-owned/-managed business.

Depending on the dynamics and circumstances within a family, a single individual holding both positions of chairperson and CEO can appear to be in a conflict of interest to nonactive shareholders, as it limits a further layer of checks and balances that would be present if the positions were to be separated.

As the role of the board is to oversee and ensure effective management, it becomes more difficult to hold the CEO accountable if that person is also leading the board of directors, especially when the individual is a family member!

Walid's Insights

Often where there is a family member serving as both chairperson and CEO, the remaining shareholders ask to be represented on the board and request a role as a director. In essence, the board ends up having the same composition as the shareholder assembly, thus frustrating the checks and balances required for good governance.

Certainly, some family members may have expertise to bring to the board and add value to the business as a whole; however, in a family business, families must make a conscious effort to ensure that the politics are adequately contained, in the interest of the business and of the family at large.

Terms

I am in favor of setting terms (time limits) for both board members and executives. I am also in favor of setting limits to the number of terms an individual may be asked to serve (e.g., terms of three [3] years each, renewable only once).

This would give an individual enough time to accomplish a given mission and would allow for new blood to come in and contribute.

Finally, this would prevent any "3C temptation," that is, complacency, collusion, and conflict of interest, which has become very current in our modern society.

Illustration

This chapter touches on leadership within the family business environment. The provisions below cover:

1. The chairperson of the board
2. The CEO
3. The family leader

Leadership

Note: Leadership in this context is the equivalent of the term "stewardship" that you find in some of the literature. It is about family leadership. Keeping the herd together and ensuring communication among the various elements that make up a family business system.

Leaders listen, give comfort, and ensure harmony and peace at home, and at the individual and group level.

Several functions are defined below. They could be used as a guide for appointing your own family business leaders.

Leadership Within the Family Business System

Chairperson of the Board

- The board members shall elect a chairperson from among them.
- The chairperson is responsible for the leadership of the board, ensuring it is effective, and carrying out the functions, as documented below.
- The chairperson will be the first among equals.
- The chairperson shall commit the time to carry out their role effectively.

Chairperson's Role Description

- The principal role of the chairperson of the board is to manage and provide leadership to the board. The chairperson acts as a direct liaison between the board and the management, through the CEO.
- More specifically, the duties and responsibilities of the chairperson shall be to:
  - chair meetings of the board and of shareholder assemblies;
  - develop and set the agenda for board and shareholder meetings, in conjunction with the CEO;
  - provide independent advice and counsel to the CEO;
  - keep abreast generally of the activities of the business;
  - act as a liaison between the board and the CEO;
  - lead the board in all aspects of its work;
  - manage effectively the affairs of the board and ensure it is suitably organized to operate effectively;
  - ensure that all board members are adequately informed to form appropriate judgments;

o monitor the implementation and enforcement of corporate governance policies;

o advise the CEO on all matters of interest to the board;

o oversee the formal succession plan for the board, the CEO, and key C-suite executives;

o identify and participate in selecting board members;

o oversee the continuing education of the board; and

o ensure the liaison with the family leader.

The CEO

- The CEO shall be appointed by the board to lead and manage the business.

- The CEO shall be responsible for the day-to-day management of the business, in line with the strategy and long-term objectives as set out and approved by the board. The CEO shall make decisions on all matters affecting the operations, performance and strategy of the business, with the exception of those matters reserved for the board or the family shareholders (reserved matters).

- The CEO shall report to the board on the strategic direction of the business.

- The CEO shall discuss with the board the annual business plan for the business. Once adopted, the CEO shall be responsible for its implementation and delivery and shall report to the board on progress at frequent and regular intervals.

- All members of the executive management team shall report directly to the CEO.

- The CEO shall represent the business to all external audiences. The CEO shall take the responsibility for the maintenance and development of the business's reputation and relationships with the media, regulators, governments, local communities, suppliers, customers, trade bodies, and other stakeholders.

Reporting to Shareholders

Note: Keeping the channels of communication open is paramount. Management should at all costs avoid surprising the shareholders with any news, whether good or bad. Periodic reporting is healthy and will consolidate the trust among individuals.

- We consider the following attributes to be hallmarks of good practice in the preparation of reports to shareholders, and as such would like to ensure that all information is communicated in adherence with the following principles:
  Clear—Reports shall be written in plain English with a simple layout so that key messages are easily identifiable.
  Consistent—The format of all reports shall be consistent so that family members are able to make easy comparisons with reports from prior periods.
  Straightforward—All reports to shareholders shall be written with the assumption that shareholders are not industry or finance experts.
  Succinct—Narratives shall be concise and to-the-point.

Annual Report to Shareholders

- We understand that when separating ownership from management, our role as shareholders becomes somewhat diminished by virtue of the fact that we have delegated to a board the management, direction, and oversight of the affairs of the business (though certain matters defined as reserved matters will remain within our remit as shareholders).
- However, while some of us may not necessarily be involved in the operational side of the business, we still wish to receive information on key matters relating to the business, as documented below.
- As shareholders, we expect to receive an annual report by [December 31] each year that includes information on the items listed below:

Business description—An outline of each of the business activities the business engages in;

Strategies—An outline of the business strategy and the results it seeks to achieve and how it plans to achieve them;

Performance highlights—A summary of KPIs and other significant highlights of the performance of the business for at least the last five (5) years in order for us to be able to make comparisons;

Chairperson and CEO statements—Direct communication from the chairperson and from the CEO putting into context the actual performance of the business against the forecasted performance;

Management—Information about who is running the business, how they are performing, and how they are remunerated; and

Shareholder information—Key dates of relevance to shareholders, a glossary of terms and metrics used throughout the report, and the key contacts able to provide further information.

Management

- It is important for us as shareholders to know the people behind the business. As such, we would like to be kept informed on the following matters:
  - o Name/title/experience/qualifications of key executives; and
  - o Name/experience/qualifications of directors.

Shareholder Information

- It is important for shareholders to have the opportunity to seek clarification and further information with respect to items in the annual report of the business. As such, we would like to receive information on the following:
  - o Contact details for queries
  - o Key dates of shareholder meetings, results announcements, record dates for dividends, the expected dates for actual dividend payments

o Any other information of particular significance to the shareholders.

Leadership Within the Family System

The Family Leader

- We recognize that the family requires a leadership champion "family leader" within and among the family to support family unity and develop the family ownership advantage.
- The family leader shall be the driving force in ensuring that the family at all times lives the values and vision of the family, the rules as prescribed in the family charter are adhered to, fair play exists at all times, meetings are properly held, and above all, that unity in the family is maintained.
- The family leader shall be responsible for ensuring an effective communication policy.
- They are the face of the family to the outside world and shall be the only person empowered to speak publicly on behalf of the family.
- Once elected by the family assembly, the term of the family leader shall be three (3) years, renewable only twice.

The Role and Profile of the Family Leader

General

- We recognize that the family can equally lead to the success or downfall of the family business.
- Therefore it is important for the family leader to work in tandem with the business leader to be the main communicator between the family and the business.
- To this end, it is important for the family leader to provide leadership, energy, motivation, and ideas while also employing resources so the family can be more effective.
- In their capacity, the family leader shall act as chairperson of the family assembly.

Desirable Characteristics of the Family Leader

- The role of the family leader is multidimensional and as such:
  - o Good interpersonal skills are critical, as they manage the family dynamics. This includes having a keen knowledge of and interest in family relationships and how individual members interact with one another, which is especially key when working between different generations. The family leader would be required to incorporate the various generational perspectives into the decision-making.
  - o The family leader shall have a true sense of purpose, responsibility, and stewardship concerning the best interests of the family as a whole and the business. They will give their time and energy but will also empower others to be engaged in the business.
  - o The family leader shall be responsible for asking the essential question: What is the goal for owning this family business? Based on the family's response, the family leader shall be responsible for developing and evolving the family's vision.
  - o The family leader shall work constructively through challenges and shall engage the family to resolve difficult situations collectively.

- The family leader shall:
  - o be highly respected by family members;
  - o uphold the values of the family;
  - o understand and defend the needs of the family;
  - o have a strong vision for the family;
  - o be objective;
  - o be an effective communicator;
  - o be a leader;
  - o be sensitive to the difficult issues within the family; and
  - o have the ability to listen to and support family members.

Reporting to Family Members

- We wish to ensure that a link is maintained between the business and the family given that the two (2) systems are not mutually exclusive.
- [This is a particularly important requirement, as in our case, the business carries the family name ("the family name") to which we as family members are directly associated.]
- In essence, our name has become a brand name and as such, the family members have certain rights with respect to their entitlement to know what is happening with the business. However, such information shall not be as detailed as the information shareholders shall be entitled to receive.
- Notwithstanding the above, it is expected that the board and the CEO shall report on key matters of the business that may have an impact on the shareholders and these shall be communicated through the family leader; such matters include but are not limited to:
  - o Any media reports and publicity that will positively/negatively impact the family name including information on the business, the board, employees and executives, and all other stakeholders the business and the board interact with
  - o Any controversial or contentious investments being considered/planned/undertaken by the business
  - o The overall financial value of the business
  - o Any other material information that may potentially affect family members or the family name.
- In essence, it is important for us that family members (where possible) receive information from the business, the shareholders, and the board directly prior to such information being disseminated or published in a public sphere. For example, in the unlikely event that the business is attached to a corporate scandal, family members should be made aware prior to any publication in the newspaper or public forum.

- Notwithstanding the above, no family member shall speak publicly on behalf of the family business or the family, nor shall a family member represent the family business or the family, with the exception of the family leader, chairperson of the board, and where appropriate, the CEO.

Section 4: Family Member Employment

Avoiding the Pitfalls

This discussion is not limited to NextGen. It also applies to board members and senior executives, including CEOs, and other C-suite family members.

Just as there is often a battle over emotion and reason in the family business, it transpires even in the field of the inclusion and employment of family members.

In many family businesses, the pursuit to continue a legacy is what keeps the family going, be it upholding the legacy of the founder, the family name, the family itself, or even flying the flag of the country, region, or city the business reigns from. After all, a family business is intertwined with the family identity. Thus the pursuit is personal, and emotional, and something that often transpires when it comes to employment matters in the family.

A common sentiment when working with families in business is that the employment of family member employees should take preference over non-family employees. In our work, we often hear the following:

There is often an assumption or a perceived duty that because we are a family business we ought to employ our own family members; there are various reasons that contribute to this ideal, though I have often found the beliefs that have contributed to this way of thinking are that:

1. *Our family business is based upon our personal relationships with suppliers, customers, and all stakeholders; therefore, we need a family member to hold and maintain these relationships;*
2. *Family members are more trustworthy; and*
3. *Family members will be better employees and work harder because they have a vested interest in the success of the business.*

On the face of it, these reasons are all valid; however, employing family members is not the sole solution for families in business. Should it be deemed that family members are not capable of being employed in the business, there are various systems and policies that can be put in place in order to neutralize the "threats" of having no family employees or management in the business. On the flip side, policies that apply to all can also be put in place stipulating the conditions of employment to regulate the inclusion of family members in the family business, ensuring that only professionally competent and capable family members can be employed.

Either way, it is important to note that a family member does not have to be working in the family business to contribute.

A family business is not a charitable organization. It is a commercial enterprise whose primary objective is to grow and generate profits. Shareholders should employ the most qualified individuals to help generate the highest return on investment, whether family or non-family.

What applies to listed companies should apply to privately held family businesses. Management is accountable to the shareholders for results. It is easier to dismiss a non-family member if they make a mistake, than it is to dismiss a brother, a cousin, or a nephew.

Furthermore, valuable employees are hard to come by. They look for career development and are ambitious. They ought to be treated with respect and they need to be taken seriously. Meritocracy should apply across the board. They will be the first ones to go should they become frustrated, or should they feel they are being treated unfairly, or even if they feel a less qualified family member is treated better than they are simply because they are family members.

Small doses of nepotism are good. It still has its place in a family business; however, the rules ought to be transparent, and managing the expectations of non-family employees should be a priority when family employees are around.

The Don'ts of Family Business Employment

1. Don't compare the NextGen/successive generations to the founders.
2. Don't compromise rounded career growth (the capacity for experience or growth) of family members (in or outside the business) for instant power and authority.

3. Don't expect the NextGen to follow your path/dream/vision for the family business, and don't impose this on them either.
4. Don't destabilize or threaten professional, experienced, and valuable non-family employees while empowering the NextGen.
5. Don't allow mature and long-standing employees who may often have allegiances to the current generation to destabilize, threaten, or obstruct the NextGen who may wish to enter the business.
6. Don't give titles without job descriptions, the necessary authority, and elbow room to operate.

The Forgotten Heroes

This refers to those family members who have been drafted to support the founding members of the business during a startup or a transition phase. They work countless hours, sacrifice their personal ambitions for the greater good, and in most cases for low or no pay.

As they watch the business grow, they miss out on proper career trajectories. They watch helplessly while other non-family employees grow within the system, and in many cases they are passed over when the time comes to promote or appoint senior managers and executives.

They are the ones I call the forgotten heroes. They feel they were taken for granted and that their contributions were not properly acknowledged.

This is a typical case of crossed wires, and missed opportunities.

The founding partners unconsciously treated those family members as owners, while the latter see themselves as mere employees.

The parties simply forgot to talk to one another and set expectations. In the meantime, their children grow up, and if not informed properly will question the status quo, and inadvertently cause pain.

The Jesuit Doctrine

Some families have adopted what I like to call the "Jesuit doctrine."

They are owners. They belong to a family business with strong values and a set of rules, applicable to all, without exception.

They de-possess themselves of everything and dedicate their lives to serving the family business. They do not have assigned jobs or titles, and they would do whatever it takes to ensure the business is successful and its values are preserved.

In exchange they, their family, and their needs are taken care of.

One day a Jesuit priest is appointed cook, the next day he may be appointed headmaster of a school, the third day he may be assigned teaching or gardening, or house-cleaning duties.

Applying the Jesuit doctrine does not happen by magic. It requires a certain mindset and upbringing. Most importantly, it requires the buy-in of all concerned.

Illustration
Family Member Employment

Note: This topic is known to raise sensitivities among family members. It is advisable that, early on, the family discusses the employment of their members in the business. Some families advocate that the business is there to support the family and that every family member is welcome to join and try their luck. Others are stricter and advocate that no family members will ever work in the business. Others even demand that the principles of meritocracy reign supreme. Some even demand that those family members who wish to join should have worked elsewhere outside the family business for a number of years before joining.

There is no sacrosanct rule. Every family needs to discuss the matter rationally and figure out what is best for its equilibrium and its happiness.

At the end of the day, the family business is an investment. It must be run by professionals, whether family members or not. It is up to the family to set the rules of employment for its members, but it should keep in mind that at the end of the day, family members are a resource and the business is an investment. Always choose the most qualified individuals to run your business (see Figure 2.5).

Family Employment: Items to Consider

Is entry into the business a birthright?

Are there any special terms and conditions of employment for family members that do not apply to non-family member employees?

Employment of in-laws?

How do you wish to reward family members?

  Pay below market rate and supplement with cash?
  Pay above market rate?
  Do not differentiate between family-member and non-family-member employees?

How will family-member appraisals be handled?

If there are no vacancies in the family business, should the business create a role for family members?

Will family members working within the business report directly to other family members?

Should family members wishing to occupy positions within the business have specific education, qualifications, character and experience?

Is the CEO to be a family member?

  Should there be a retirement age? If yes, what should it be?

  Are family members who work full-time in the business allowed to have passive interests in non-competing businesses as long as it is not a conflict of time and their commitment to the business? Before a family member employed in the business makes a passive interest, should this be disclosed?

Figure 2.5

Principles of Family Employment

- We are committed to owning a professionally run family business. Therefore, the best interests of the group will always be taken into account before the interests of one (1) or more individual family members in relation to employment decisions.
- We would like to attract the most talented and qualified people for key positions, regardless of their family membership.
- Employment in the business is neither a birthright of family members, nor an obligation, although we acknowledge that in order to maintain the family business nature of the business, there will ideally be family members working therein.
- [Spouses, however, who are non-bloodline are not permitted to be employed in the family business.]
- [We believe that the experience of working in different organizations is important for family members who work in the family business. As such, family members will be considered for employment in the business once they have acquired at least five (5) years of relevant outside experience (in which they achieved highly and progressed).]
- It is expected that family members employed by the business will set an example to others through their dedication, performance, and conduct.

- It is acknowledged that being a family member does not automatically create an expectation of seniority within the business, and that all family members must work their way up through the business, as appropriate.
- We will only provide job opportunities commensurate with each individual's skillset, ability, and qualifications.
- We wish for the family to benefit from the business and where appropriate enjoy employment in the family business. There are important foundations to employment with the business and the family's interaction with the business:
  1. We do not want to create two (2) classes of employees—family vs. non-family. As such, no special conditions or favors will be given to family members over non-family members. This is due to the fact that we do not want to disengage non-family members working in the group.
  2. While related party transactions may occur between the business and family members, we will not award contracts purely based on the fact that the contractor is a family member. Contracts will be awarded on merit.
- Family members employed in the business will receive the same salary and benefits as non-family members employed in the same position would.
- We will never create a role specifically for a family member—there must be a clear business need for any family member working in the business.
- Family members employed by the business will be required to abide by the employment policies of the business and to this end will be required to sign and adhere to an employment contract that will include provisions on the terms of employment, as well as a non-competition and non-solicitation provision.

Procedure for Family Employment

- A family member wishing to work in the business ("the applicant") may file an application ("the application") with the assistance of the family leader, to be submitted to the board. It is left to the discretion of the board to determine whether the applicant should be considered for a position in the business.
- Should the board consider the application suitable and the applicant desirable, the chairperson shall submit the application to the CEO. The CEO shall forward the application to the Human Resources Department ("the HR Department").
- The HR department will help the applicant consider potential areas of the business that may be the best fit for them. The HR department will also assist candidates with ensuring they have the requisite skills and qualifications for any potential role.
- If employed, all family members must produce a career-development plan, in conjunction with the HR department, to ensure that they continue to meet the expectations of the business and progress in their career.
- Family members working in the business must be appraised and overseen by a non-family member mentor, and no HR-related decisions may be made by immediate family members of any applicant.

Family Member Participation on the Board

- We recognize that family shareholders and family members may not always have the skills and proficiencies that would be most beneficial to the board and the business.
- As such, family members may only join the board or its committees based on merit and their capabilities, and any family member striving to gain entry to the board and its committees must (at a minimum):
  - o Have five (5) years prior board experience
  - o Be passionate about the group and demonstrate dedication

o Be able to contribute the time and professional skills to help oversee the group while understanding that the role is to focus on strategic issues.

Training, Education, and Development Policy

- The board shall be responsible for working with the HR department to ensure the assignment of mentors or coaches from the business to ensure for family members appropriate work experience, in-house training, and development, alongside any outsourced training, development, or formal education for family members.
- There are many tools to apply in support of family members' careers, before or during their employment with the business, which shall all be considered for implementation on a case-by-case basis for each family member:

Mentors or coaches: Experienced, skilled group executive management and management can spend time with the NextGen leader on a regular basis. They provide a mix of support and challenge to help the individual reach their full potential.

360-degree feedback: Ensure feedback for family members and from managers, peers, and subordinates. This could be ensured by them completing questionnaires about the performance of family members. Based on the feedback, the individual completes a learning plan that specifies how they will strengthen weaknesses and capitalize on strengths.

Individual learning plans: Written goals and timetables for personal development help ensure that the individual really follows through.

Note: Some family members look for security in the form of "lifetime" employment. In this case, I would suggest to look to the family office for such support, as opposed to the family business.

Depleting the resources of the family business for short-term gains will be detrimental in the long term. Embracing family members and providing them with security is a job the family office can take on.

"One for all, and all for one" is a concept the family should collectively discuss and embrace, if they want to.

Section 5: Family Office

This section will discuss family offices as a tool used to separate family affairs from business affairs. It deals with the most basic approach.

Many of the aspects discussed below may not apply to a family that has sold its business and has come into massive liquidity and has decided to set up a fund to invest such liquidity to generate wealth and sustain the needs of the family.

What Is a Family Office?

For me, a family office is the ultimate tool that affirms the separation of business affairs from family affairs (see Figure 2.6).

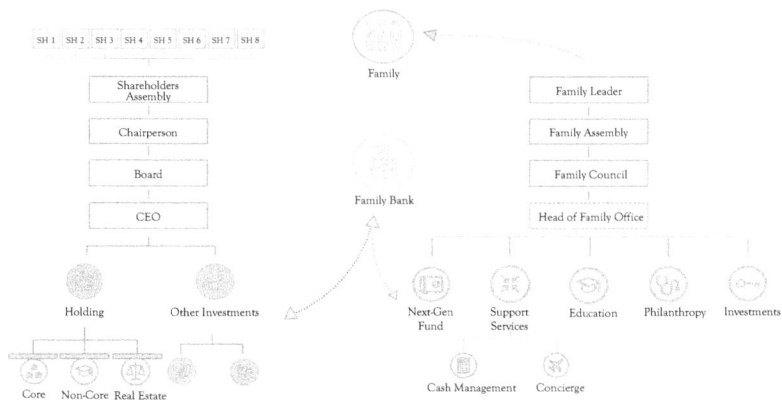

Figure 2.6

There is no single defined activity or definition for a family office; however, I like to use the family office, in the early stages of a succession plan, as a tool to preserve the family legacy and manage and grow the family's wealth in all its forms:

- Intellectual
- Cultural
- Human
- Financial
- Social

In order to meet these objectives, a family office should be built according to what a given family feels it needs or expects from a family office. Accordingly, the structure within a family office should be determined by, and be reflective of, each family member's individual needs.

The family office will serve the family's own interests. The goals and objectives of the family in ascertaining what they require from the family office will be essential to building it, whether the objective is to

- increase the family's income;
- fulfill lifestyle requirements; or
- keep the family connected.

It is rare to find a family that can set up a Bessemer-, Quilvest-, or Rockefeller-type family office structure overnight.

Most start modestly and develop their family office infrastructure as the family matures and its appetite for risk grows.

These factors shall all affect the role and structure of the family office.

The most crucial element of any family office is that it will operate independently from the business, thus ensuring a separation between the family system and the business system.

Because the beneficial owners of a family office are the family itself, the use of its services will constantly be scrutinized. This reality makes the task of defining the raison d'être, the values system, and the profile of the professionals who are going to help the family run the family office much more difficult tasks.

In addition to being highly qualified at what they do, professionals who work with family businesses must be quick-witted and adept at reading between the lines. Appearances may be deceiving: They may think that they report to one person in the family, but in reality, the entire family is their client. Should a professional alienate one member, they risk losing their job. It is important for them to remember that they are not friends of the family—they are employees, whose task is to get the job done. For this reason, it is crucial that they remain neutral and treat all family members equally. They should never take sides or judge, and should take care to keep in mind the old adage that blood is thicker than water.

This being said, a family office may still serve to assist the business requirements of family members for business matters that are independent of the family business; for example, investment banking or other new business ventures which family members may wish to undertake individually or jointly (see Figure 2.7).

Ultimate Objectives of a Family Office

In my experience working with family offices, they are often built with the purpose of addressing the following five main areas:

Family Governance
- Preservation of family legacy
- Level the field among family members and secure fairness and harmony among them
- Organize the relationship among family members and their relationship with the source of financial wealth

Corporate Governance
- Secure a successful transition from autocracy to democracy
- Agree on a succession plan at executive and management levels
- Ensure sustainability of the group in the hands of Next-Gen shareholders

Financial Governance
- Preserve and grow wealth
- Avoid ownership fragmentation upon the passing of the owners
- Devise an estate planning strategy (inheritance) to ensure the orderly transfer of ownership

Risk Mitigation
- Manage risks in relation to the family, business, and investments
- Manage family risks, including identity theft and family name protection
- Manage all legal, tax, and inheritance risks

- Effective succession planning to ensure the sustainability of the family wealth
- Ring-fence assets
- Physical security

Next-Gen Succession
- Prepare the Next-Gen to enable them to take over the group
- Introduce the Next-Gen, where possible, develop a role for them, particularly while there is still an opportunity to learn from and work with the senior generation

- Determine the time frame for starting the process
- Empower the Next-Gen for continued family cohesiveness

Figure 2.7

Walid's Insights

Family (investment) offices are commonly formed following a liquidity event, or when the founding generations (G1) or G2 have developed a significantly prosperous business and they wish to serve the needs and requirements of the family to a standard they feel they deserve.

Further, they often wish to use it as a tool to diversify their investments and support the NextGen in their individual business endeavors.

At its inception, a family office usually provides concierge and lifestyle services to the family and as the family evolves it evolves with them.

Very often the family office institutionalizes services that are already provided to the family by the business, and this is a first step toward the separation of family affairs from business affairs.

Services Provided by a Family Office

As a general rule, a family office can do whatever you like it to do. The services outlined in Figure 2.8 are the most common.

Wealth Management
- Asset management / allocation
- Private equity portfolio
- Commodities portfolio
- Aircraft consulting
- Art investment
- External manager selection
- Monitoring & reporting

Investment Strategy
- "Family bank"
- Portfolio revaluation
- Venture capital
- Investment banking
- IPO
- Private placement
- Sharia compliant structures

Philanthropy
- Performance philanthropy
- Family foundations
- Zakat

Planning
- Estate planning
- Tax planning
- Financial planning

Risk Management/Asset Protection
- Liability management
- Debt structure & analysis/ bank financing
- Convenient and competitive banking services
- Physical (travel) security
- ID/name protection
- Insurance

Banking Services
- Retail banking
- Elite banking
- SMEs
- Credit card
- Credit risk

Keeping Fingers on the Pulse
- Identify needs and concerns
- Long-term vision
- Individual ambitions
- Family values
- Ensure alignment with vision

Family Governance
- Family constitution
- Family councils
- Family representatives
- Exit strategies
- Retirement plans
- Pension funds
- Conflict resolution/ management

Family Well-being
- Health care
- Education
- Training
- Coaching
- Entertainment

Corporate Governance
- Corporate re-engineering/ legal structures
- Separation of ownership from management
- Shareholders agreements
- Board of managers
- Empowerment
- Transparency and accountability

Concierge
- Bill payment and payroll management
- Book-keeping
- Cash-flow management
- Private property management
- Personal travel management
- Collectibles
- Luxury toys management

Figure 2.8

A serious conversation must take place at the family level to determine the needs, the costs, and the benefit of setting up a family office.

Depending on what the family needs, the family office will be given a name, such as "Investment House," "Family Support Services Desk," and so on.

Structure of a Family Office

Once the family has determined and understood the mission of the family office, the family can then engage advisors to determine the most effective corporate and legal structure for the family office. In this regard, it is important to assess:

- The corporate structuring of the family office
- The jurisdiction of the family office
- The legal structure of the family office (e.g., corporation, partnership, limited liability company, etc.)
- The tax implications: the need to set up a trust, a private trust company, a foundation, and so on.
- What activities are to be carried out in-house vs. those that will be outsourced

- The manner in which the office will be governed and monitored
- Reporting mechanism to the family

Commonly, as families grow, so do their assets and investments. The structure of their family offices will adapt accordingly.

An example of a family office structure we have seen is outlined in Figure 2.9.

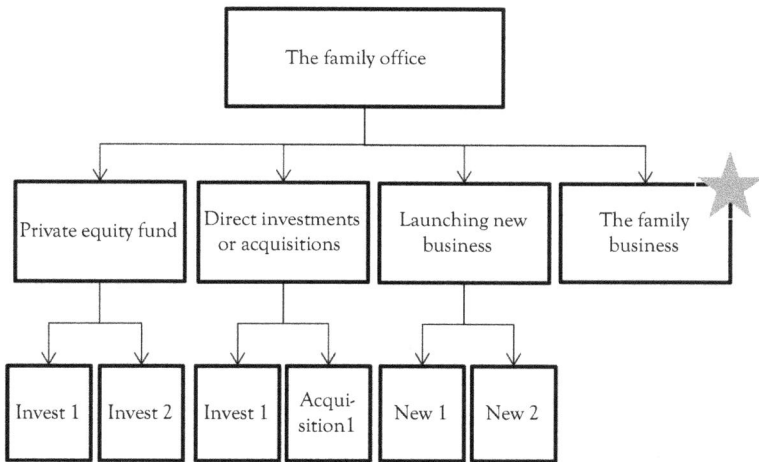

Figure 2.9

What was once the main and only source of income for the family transforms into another investment, particularly as the business is passed through the generations and the personal (emotional) attachment to the business becomes less and less apparent.

Family Finances and the Financing of the Family Office

Having made the decision to build a family office and having determined the services the family would require from a family office, the financial framework around the same must be built.

Financing the activities of a family office is often a subject of discord.

It is advisable that, early on, families discuss what it is that they expect their family office to offer them, who is going to manage it, and how they are planning to finance its activities.

Typically, a family office is funded as outlined in Figure 2.10.

Family Office Flow of Funds

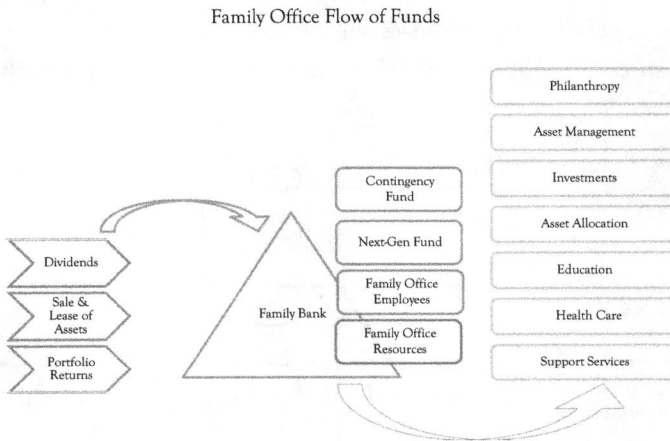

Figure 2.10

Walid's Insights

A family office can be a powerful tool. It is recommended that a family that decides to separate its business affairs from its personal affairs engages in a serious conversation regarding the purpose of establishing such a tool, the objectives it wishes to achieve, and the values system driving it.

Once this exercise is complete, it will become easier to define the profile of the team who will work at the family office, and that of its leader. It will also help better frame the services delivered and activities undertaken by the family office.

The functions, frameworks, and objectives of family offices differ greatly from one family to another. The concept of a family office, as it is implemeted today, is still is in its infancy, and I believe that it is premature at this stage to offer any sample provisions for a family office.

To do sufficient justice to this topic would warrant writing another book, perhaps in a few years, that deals exclusively with this subject.

Conclusion

Choose a job you love, and you never have to work a day in your life.
—Confucius

I had a fabulous time writing this book. I hope you found its content useful, and I hope it helped you appreciate what is at stake over the next 10–20 years and beyond.

Every line I wrote reminded me of a situation that I lived through with the families who took me into their confidence and trusted me. It has been both an honor and a pleasure serving them.

Working alongside some of the most influential business families is in itself gratifying and above all, educational. Not only did I have access to individuals who control assets worth hundreds of billions of dollars, but I also had access to visionaries who have the ability to influence the course of events that shape the business world. Besides being change agents themselves, their businesses are the backbone of the economy. They are the employers of choice for hundreds of thousands of individuals, and they contribute significantly to the GDP of their respective countries.

Family businesses are the combined heartbeat and the soul of most modern economies.

Beyond the theory that lies behind the interaction of the various systems, the generational transitions, and the textbook scenarios of the omnipresent patriarch/matriarch and the continually questioning Next-Gen, you get to see firsthand what really goes on behind the scenes.

I learned that in most circumstances, all is not what meets the eye. In a family business, what you see is not necessarily what you get. I have learned that, in a family business, the adviser has to tear away many layers of concealment to get to the truth. Those who conceal things in corporations do so almost entirely for personal gain. The motivation to conceal things within a family business can be for many reasons—for fear of embarrassment, or purely as a result of a desire to uphold the prestige of one part of the family and to not lose face. It is a complex picture.

The activities of families in business are a convoluted web of relationships, and an intricate balancing act to meet the competing needs of all stakeholders. This includes the entire gambit of family owners, suppliers, customers, employees, partners, governments, and so on.

Getting this balance right affects the operation of entities, establishments, individuals, corporations, and communities at all levels. Observing this interaction and learning about the different roles that are assumed and the tools that are employed enables you to look at their world in a holistic manner.

You realize that everything happens for a reason. There is also a reason for what does not happen.

You learn to appreciate how legal concepts are developed, how government policies are devised, and how business decisions are made.

You cease to judge and instead, you learn to observe, to analyze, and to anticipate. You have no power to change the things that need to be changed. You must build a relationship of trust that enables you to influence those who can change things for the benefit of all.

In theory, this seems straightforward, but in practice, it is much more complex. It demands, perseverance, patience, and passion.

I sometimes compare it to artisanship.

Science teaches you to "know," while the art teaches you to "understand."

As with any professional activity, family business advisory has a science and an art element to it. The science can be learned and taught, but the art and the mastery come with time, experience, empathy, and thinking outside the box.

The practice of family business advisory as a "profession" was relatively nascent when I embarked on this career. Over the years the practice has evolved significantly and a remarkable amount of interest has developed around it, reflecting the growing importance of family businesses around the globe. While there remains room for study and development of family business succession planning, today we have access to a great deal of material, studies, and statistics covering families in business.

With this being said, when you are immersed in the practice, you learn that families in business are not mere statistics. If you serve them properly, your role extends far beyond that of an advisor. You are their confidant, their trusted advisor, and part of the extended family.

Once you prove yourself and earn that position of trust, you have to work hard to maintain your integrity and your place alongside those at the top table, and that comes from the delivery of excellence.

Delivery of excellence does not only occur in the solutions you offer. Much more critical than what you deliver is the way you deliver it. Your personal integrity and conduct are paramount.

It has been my privilege, over many years, to have had such access to the families with whom I have worked, from the founders to the upcoming generations. I am grateful for the trust these families have placed in me and in my team through this hugely rewarding and enjoyable journey.

Walid S. Chiniara
March 2020

About the Author

Walid S. Chiniara is an international finance lawyer, a leading expert, and a recognized pioneer in matters pertaining to legal strategy, governance, and dynastic planning for family enterprises. In 2021, Walid will celebrate 40 years of practicing law across five continents. 24 of those years would have been spent serving elite business families in his capacity as a trusted advisor and a mediator managing intergenerational conflicts within a family business context. Over time, Walid has forged himself a reputation as the go-to person for mission-impossible family business succession planning.

Index

Letter 'f' after page number indicates figure.

OTHER TITLES IN THE ENTREPRENEURSHIP AND SMALL BUSINESS MANAGEMENT COLLECTION

Scott Shane, Case Western University, Editors

- *How to Succeed as a Solo Consultant* by Stephen D. Field
- *Small Business Management* by Andreas Karaoulanis
- *Native American Entrepreneurs* by Ron P. Sheffield and Munoz J. Mark
- *The Entrepreneurial Adventure* by David James and Oliver James
- *On All Cylinders, Second Edition* by Ron Robinson
- *Cultivating an Entrepreneurial Mindset* by Tamiko L. Cuellar
- *From Vision to Decision* by Dana K. Dwyer
- *Get on Board* by Olga V. Mack
- *The Rainmaker* by Jacques Magliolo
- *Department of Startup* by Ivan Yong Wei Kit and Sam Lee

Announcing the Business Expert Press Digital Library

Concise e-books business students need for classroom and research

This book can also be purchased in an e-book collection by your library as

- a one-time purchase,
- that is owned forever,
- allows for simultaneous readers,
- has no restrictions on printing, and
- can be downloaded as PDFs from within the library community.

Our digital library collections are a great solution to beat the rising cost of textbooks. E-books can be loaded into their course management systems or onto students' e-book readers.
The **Business Expert Press** digital libraries are very affordable, with no obligation to buy in future years. For more information, please visit **www.businessexpertpress.com/librarians**. To set up a trial in the United States, please email **sales@businessexpertpress.com**.